HAWK

HAWK

BY KEN HARRELSON

WITH AL HIRSHBERG

NEW YORK / THE VIKING PRESS

CONTENTS

Illustrations follow page 88

HAWK

1 | The Nose Makes the Man

"You handsome sonofagun, don't you ever die!"

I look in the mirror and say that anywhere from one to a dozen times a day, depending on how often I shave, change my clothes, comb my hair, or just happen to see my reflection somewhere. It may sound a little conceited, but that's neither here nor there. When I spot the ensemble, especially the nose that goes with it, I can't help myself.

For there's no doubt about it—the nose makes the man. Nosewise, the Hawk is the noblest Roman of them all. You can talk about Caesar, Cyrano, Durante, or any of those other jokers, but they're pikers compared to me. My nose is my bag, my trademark, my thing, my life. It makes me what I am today—not just a big-league ballplayer named Ken Harrelson (baseball is my worst sport anyhow), but a character universally known as Hawk—*the* Hawk. There are at least two other Harrelsons in professional baseball. The world is full of Kens. But how many Hawks are there?

Which is why "Hawk" is embroidered, embossed, engraved, embedded, impressed, or printed on practically everything I own. You'll find it on my slacks, my sweaters, my shirts, my jackets, my underwear, my baseball gear, my stationery, and my car. You'll even find it tiled on the walls of the bathroom of my apartment in the Boston suburb of Brookline.

And all on account of my nose. I wouldn't be so proud of it if it had just happened to come with the rest of me, but I earned it the hard way. The nose I was born with was pretty straight. Had a little hump on the bridge, but nothing that you'd notice unless you looked for it. Then, when I was seven or eight—something like that—it got broken the first time. That happened while I was watching a baseball game in Woodruff, South Carolina, where I was born, maybe a couple of years before we left there.

Man, I wanted to get into that game the worst way, but the kids told me I was too small. Somewhere along the line somebody had to go home, so one of the boys handed me a bat and told me I'd be up next. I crouched in what would have been the on-deck circle, just the way I'd seen big leaguers do on television, and waited for the guy ahead of me to hit. When he did, he slung the bat and ran. I was watching the ball, didn't see the damn bat coming, and it hit me right across the face.

I want to tell you, it just shattered my nose. I could feel the bumps and cracks in it without touching it. With all the blood and tears, I didn't know much of anything for a little while, then the only thing I could think of was what my mama would say. By the time I realized what was going on, one of the older kids was bending over me. When he touched my nose, I jumped five feet, it hurt so much. I guess a couple of others held me while he yanked it back into place. Believe me, the tears were really streaming then. It hurt like hell. And the ground where I was sitting, and my clothes, and everything around me were a bloody mess.

They finally got me calmed down and cleaned up a little and I started home, wondering what the hell I was going to say. I couldn't hide my nose. It was swelled up something terrible. My mama took one look and cried, "What happened? You poor kid! What happened?"

It never occurred to me to tell her the truth. I was afraid she'd be mad if she knew I was careless enough to let myself get hit by a baseball bat. So I said, "I got into a fight."

She was too worried to be mad. She just reached out and stroked my nose a little, and sort of cooed, but all I could do was stand there and try to keep from busting out crying. It killed me when she touched it, but I didn't want to tell her how much it hurt.

From then on, especially at that age, my face was all nose. Nothing else counted—my eyes, my forehead, my cheeks, my mouth, my teeth, my chin were all smothered. Naturally, they got bigger as I got bigger, but so did my nose. No matter what else ever happened to it—and plenty did—it was forever to stand far out of proportion to the rest of my face. It was so big, in fact, that you had to look closely to notice that its tip, once nice and straight, veered a little to the left.

Just before we left Woodruff—I was in the fourth grade, I think —I broke my nose again, this time playing football. We were playing defense in a pickup game on the same playground where I got hit with the bat, and the kid with the ball was coming toward me at an angle. When I reached him and started wrestling him down, his shoulder pad, which must have been made of concrete, got me right in the nose. That time it was a clean fracture, not all shattered like the first time, but it hurt just as much. The playground director took me to the hospital, where the doctor set my nose, bound it in adhesive tape, and sent me home. That break hardly changed my nose at all. Oh, it added a little hump, but with a nose the size of mine, that didn't mean anything.

I was living in Savannah when I broke my nose the third time. This was in a fight while I was in high school. I'll tell you the details later. Anyhow, the other guy must have belted my nose a dozen times, hitting me so hard and so often that in a way he did me a favor. He smashed the tip of my nose straight. But the fight added body to my nose. Even though I now walked around with everything veering in the right direction again, my nose was bigger in all aspects—thicker, higher, longer, and beakier.

The fourth break came just the way the second did—while I was playing football. We were having a high-school game workout, with the linemen wearing bird cages and the backs bars. I was the quarterback, scrambling around trying to get off a pass, when a guy broke through and belted me in the face. My bar broke and one end of it smashed right into my nose and shattered it all to hell. That really did it. I ended up with my present nose, a gorgeous monstrosity, full and crooked and bigger than ever.

I broke my nose once more before I was through, but I'm sort of ashamed of that one. Not only was it just a little break, but it hardly changed the shape of my nose at all. It happened the year I got home to Savannah after my first season in organized baseball. I was pretty cocky—what the hell, how many guys in Savannah get bonuses for signing baseball contracts?—and maybe I sometimes got on people's nerves.

Anyhow, I dropped into an oyster bar where a lot of the kids I went to high school with hung out, and a guy I didn't know very well came over and said, "You're Ken Harrelson, aren't you?"

"You know who I am," I said. "You've seen me around here enough."

I suppose I bugged him a little the way I said it. Or maybe he was trying to impress his girl. Or maybe he was jealous because I had had a good sports career and he hadn't. Or maybe he just had been building up a thing against me all these years. Whatever it was, he suddenly reared back and popped me right on the nose. No reason—nothing—just popped me. I hit him back as sort of a reflex, a pretty good belt, if I say so myself, because it knocked him cold. While that satisfied my ego, it didn't do much for my nose. It was broken, all right, although not too badly. As I say, I'm a little ashamed of counting it, but a break is a break. So, in the interests of accuracy, I must report that I broke my nose not once, twice, three times or four, but five.

Under the circumstances, you can hardly blame me for being nose-conscious. As long as I can remember, kids called me by names inspired by that feature—Banana Nose, Hook Nose, Schnozz, Eaglebeak—you name it, I've been called it. Because I sometimes did sort of crazy things, I was also known as Nutsy. A few kids called me Spider because I was so skinny, and a couple even called me Ken. And, believe it or not, there were those who called me Hawk. But that name didn't really catch on until I got into baseball.

The guy who made it stick was Dick Howser. We were in winter ball together in 1959, the year I broke in—Dunedin, Florida, I think it was. Dick is a little guy with a big voice, and every time I came to bat you could hear him all over the field yelling, "Hawk." If I got a hit, I was "Henry Hawk"; if I didn't, "Henrietta Hawk." Pretty soon everyone was calling me Hawk, and I've been Hawk ever since.

My nose is directly responsible for my name. Indirectly, it's responsible for just about everything else about me—my clothes, my hair, my shoes, my car, my apartment, my refusal to follow the crowd, my independence, my complete departure from convention. If I had an ordinary nose, I'd be an ordinary guy—regular enough, I suppose, but nobody you'd look at twice. But with my nose, I *had* to be different, if for no other reason than to divert attention from it.

On account of my nose, I wear my hair as long as I can get away with wearing it. During the baseball season I have to shorten it a little so it will fit under a cap. During the off-season it comes down over my ears. I have the job done by pros and pay maybe twenty, twenty-five bucks for it. They give me the full treatment—razor cut, styling, shaping, shampooing, hair-netting, drying under the same kind of dryer they use in women's beauty parlors, the works. And if I don't like it when they're through, they do it all over again.

I don't see anything unusual about having my hair done right. Lots of perfectly normal, virile men like me have their hair done professionally, including a good many ballplayers I know. Why, hell, I've even had a set of pictures of myself under a dryer and with my hair in a net appear in *The Sporting News,* baseball's bible, and nobody thought anything of it. And I was under a dryer on television once, too. I'll admit ballplayers of the old days wouldn't be caught dead in poses like that, but these aren't the old days.

Come to think of it, after Babe Ruth retired from baseball he wore a big bobby pin when he played golf to keep his hair out of his eyes, and I never heard of anyone making any smart cracks about him.

Long hair only partially draws the eye away from my fantastic nose. The rest of that job is done by my clothes. I am, I admit, an absolute nut on clothes. I call mine mind-benders. Sometimes —very occasionally—I can get a mind-bender off the rack, but most of the time I design my own.

The hair and the clothes pay off, believe me. If I had a crew cut or kept my hair short, people would say, "Look at the nose on that guy." And if I dressed conventionally, they'd say, "Did you ever see such a nose?"

You know what they say now? "Look at the Hawk. What splendor! What class! What style! What perfection!"

Just to give you an idea: I showed up at a Boston Bruins hockey game one night last winter in an outfit of my own design with a touch of Nehru, a touch of Edwardian, and a nice big splash of pure Hawk. It was a gold-and-white silk-brocade suit. The jacket had a Nehru collar, but with Edwardian lapels, and the pants had twelve-inch pleats up the sides. But the *pièce de resistance* were the shoes. They were made of exactly the same material—gold-and-white silk brocade.

When I walked into the Boston Garden that night, I knocked them dead, which was just what I intended to do. After all, I didn't expect to go through a crowded arena lobby in an outfit like mine incognito.

I moved very carefully—not strutting, mind you, but not walking at my ordinary gait either. I had to use the perfect pace, casual yet regal, not too slow yet giving photographers as much time as they needed for pictures. I couldn't stop to pose. That would have been too obvious.

It worked fine. Wherever I went on my way to my seat I heard people murmur and saw them point. To a ham like me, those are supreme accolades. So you see, that outfit was cheap at three hundred and fifty bucks. It provided me with one of my finest hours.

Then there was the suit I wore for the annual Boston Baseball Writers dinner in January 1969—my first attempt to design something for formal use. I was at the head table to receive the writers' award for being the Red Sox's most valuable player in 1968, so I had to make it good.

Well, I'll be honest with you. The ensemble was a real mind-bender: white shoes, white velvet bell-bottom trousers, white velvet jacket trimmed with black velvet, and a black velvet vest. Everybody thought it was great—the ballplayers, the writers, the fans, the other head-table guests, and everyone else in the place. I wore that outfit only one other time and it set me back five hundred fish, but I didn't consider a penny of it wasted.

I made several television appearances during the winter after the 1968 baseball season, including a big program in which I was featured. Naturally, I followed script directions, but they let me pick my own clothes and pretty much do my own thing.

In general, I dressed pretty conservatively, sticking to basic styles and colors. After all, I didn't want to make a spectacle of myself. The first time I came out in a gray sweater over a white turtleneck shirt, with gray slacks and white shoes. Nothing sensational about that, is there?

Later, I appeared in a blue sateen jacket, a white pullover turtleneck, love beads, white shoes, and gray slacks with blue hairline stripes. When I came out with a singing group, I had a multicolored kerchief instead of the love beads and changed my slacks to patterned hip-huggers which were really mind-benders. Then I had to sing—a mistake, because I'm about as lousy at that as you can get—wearing a purple paisley packet and a pair of dark glasses pushed up over my hair. The rest of the outfit was white.

I did scenes with the Four Lads, with Peter, Paul and Mary, and with Tiny Tim, an avid baseball fan who surprised me with his knowledge of the game. We swapped souvenirs later. I gave him a medallion and he gave me an autographed ukulele.

The bits I liked the least about the show were some flashbacks of me indulging in other sports—playing golf, shooting pool, that sort of thing. I have no modesty about my ability as an all-round athlete because I know I'm pretty good at just about everything. Since my reactions are quick, my coordination good, and I'm physically strong, I have complete confidence in anything I try.

What bothered me about the sports bits I disliked was the way I looked. My hair was too short and I looked more clod than mod. There was even a shot of me in a hat. I once had a yen for hats, but no more. The only things that ever go on my head now are dark glasses and baseball caps.

I got big kicks out of several scenes. One was some shots of me dancing at my favorite Boston night spot, the Point After. It's owned by Gino Cappelletti of the Boston Patriots, and it's a real swinging joint. The action begins around eleven and ends when everybody drops dead.

Another bit that tickled me was the one with the hair dryer, when a gal named Margo from the Casa Burrone of Boston Barber Salon Stylists to Men invented the "Onion Hawk" right in front of the camera and everybody—in color yet. As she worked on this original style we talked about the future of men's hair-styling, a subject on which she is naturally an authority. She did most of the talking and I did practically all the agreeing, because I think she was right on almost every count. But I'm not so sure about her statement that within five years three-quarters of the men who can afford it will have their hair not only styled but dyed.

Now, I know a lot of guys who change the color of their hair when it starts to go gray, and I'll probably do that myself if I live that long, but I can't imagine men changing their hair colors on impulse the way women do. I certainly don't intend to fool around with my dirty-blond mop. I like it just the way it is. I will occasionally have Margo give me an Onion Hawk, but I'll be damned if I'll let her make a redhead or a brunette out of me.

On the show she said men are vainer than women about their appearance, and I agreed with her there. After all, I'm Exhibit A myself on that score. Margo said the present mod departures from convention are only the beginning. According to her, in another five or ten years only old fuddy-duddies will be wearing throat-choking dress shirts and suits all cut alike. Ties are already going the way of spats. Anybody who wears them will look medieval. I'll bet the time will come when a guy like me can walk through the Boston Garden lobby in elephant-skin shorts and nobody will look twice.

While talking to Margo, I had a Joe Namath type of mustache painted on—you know, that Fu Manchu thing he got ten thousand dollars for shaving off just before the Super Bowl game. I don't know if the mustache did anything for me, but I wouldn't even try to grow one. My skin is so fair and my hair so light it would take months. I do better in the big mop and sideburns, although I like to wear a phony mustache once in a while.

Before the show ended, the Val Perry Trio sang a number called "Don't Walk the Hawk," which was so flattering that even my enormous ego isn't big enough to repeat it. Although I had just led the American League in runs-batted-in and been named its player-of-the-year, I hardly qualified as a combination of Babe Ruth, Willie Mays, Joe DiMaggio, Ted Williams, Mickey Mantle, and Carl Yastrzemski, which "Don't Walk the Hawk" makes me sound like. Don't get me wrong—I loved it—but, after all, there are limits to everything.

The show ended in a golden blaze of sartorial glory. Yes, I wore that suit again, that mind-bending brocade outfit I had stopped the show with at the Bruins game.

The TV show actually murdered "Gunsmoke" in the local ratings during its first half hour and even outranked "Laugh-In" during the second, but that didn't mean anything. It appeared over a Boston outlet and was well advertised in advance. Any local big-name will outrank a national show on a one-shot deal like that. I'd like to try it again, only this time having more to say about the material. I can do a better job ad-libbing or acting as an emcee than blindly following a script I don't have a chance to check in advance.

I'm in the public eye as a ballplayer, but, since the nose made the clothes as well as the man, I wouldn't mind putting as much time into clothes as sports. After all, I'm a clothes bug—I have so much stuff I've long since lost count of it. I really need a valet when I travel, if only to keep track of my clothes and see that everything that goes to the cleaners comes back intact. Believe me, that alone is a tough job. When I take care of my own clothes, I'm the world's most careless character. Since I never know what

I have starting out and buy stuff by the ton while I'm gone, I don't know what I should still have when I get home.

One reason I lose so much is that apparently some laundry workers collect souvenirs. That HAWK embroidered on practically everything I own is too much for a light-fingered guy to resist. I must have contributed thirty sweaters to laundries during the 1968 baseball season.

I just throw everything into a bag and send it out, so naturally I don't know if it all comes back. The only time I find a sweater or a shirt missing is when I look for one to wear. I might not miss it for weeks, and then it's too late to track it down. Anyhow, who's ever going to admit he took a sweater or a shirt out of a laundry?

When I'm on the road with the ball club my cleaning bill runs at least sixty bucks per trip. Every time we hit a new town I have stuff to go out. My 1968 roommate, Jerry Adair, was appalled at the dough I spent for cleaning and pressing. He used to hang out his four suits on the shower rod in the bathroom, turn on the hot water, close the door and let 'em steam.

One day in Anaheim I said, "Does that really work?"

"Sure it does," he said. "Hell, Hawk, you're out of your mind spending so much dough at the cleaner's. Steam them the way I do. You'll save yourself thirty bucks a trip."

I decided to try it after Jerry got through. I went into the bathroom, hung up my slacks and suits and jackets, including a couple of very fancy Nehrus, filled the tub with hot water and closed the door. Later, I was sitting watching television when I heard this awful crash. The damn shower rod had broken and all my beautiful clothes were in the water. That was the last time I tried to save money Adair's way.

You can't save money if you want a really spectacular wardrobe. That's why I never had one until I came to the Red Sox in 1967. They gave me a huge bonus to sign after Charley Finley, the Athletics owner, let me sell my services to the highest bidder by firing

13

me. Sensible people—yes, even style nuts like me—blanch at the thought of the dough I spent for clothes after arriving in Boston. I figure I blew about ten thousand dollars.

Now, that's really a hell of a lot of money to spend on anything in so short a time. But, hell, man, I grew up loving clothes and never having the money to pay for the kind I really wanted. Oh, I dressed well enough—even as a kid when we were broke I always looked neat and decent. But ten Gs in six months?

Yet I think it was justified. In the first place, I could afford it. In the second, I could attract national attention out of Boston, where a good deal of the action is. Kansas City is a great town, but nobody cares much what happens there except other people in Kansas City. Besides, I was a .230 hitter in Kansas City. In Boston, with its nice close leftfield fence built for right-handed hitters like me, I suddenly became a slugger.

That Red Sox bonus enabled me to spend real money on clothes, but even at Kansas City I was hardly a shrinking violet—not spectacular, you understand, but good enough to get by. In those days, I guess I spent a couple of thousand a year for clothes. That's not bad, I suppose, but I don't see how a guy who travels much can get by for less.

Clothes wear out fast on the road. Just moving them around, either on your back or on racks or in suitcases, takes something out of them. And cleaning is not only expensive but murder on them. Every time something goes to the cleaners it loses a little, and pretty soon it has to go into the ash can.

Maybe other people can keep stuff for years, but I can't—at least not often. The only thing I ever had that lasted was a blue sports coat I bought in Savannah in 1959 when I was seventeen years old. Man, I loved that jacket. It was a shade of blue I've seen maybe only ten times in all the years since. I've gone through several pairs of slacks that I bought especially to wear with it, and it was like losing a close relative when I had to throw it away last year. I rarely had it cleaned. That's why it lasted so long. I wish I could find another like it, but in years of prowling shops all over the country I never have.

I'm a compulsive shopper. When I'm on the road with the ball club, I'm out of the room by ten or ten-thirty so I can wander around looking for stuff. I used to leave town with enough room in my luggage for anything new I might happen to pick up. Until this year I had a couple of suitcases and a clothes rack, but now I use a trunk. It's half empty at the start of a trip and full at the finish. I'm a real nut for sweaters and slacks. I buy them by the dozen, and sometimes junk them without wearing them. What looks great in a store doesn't always stand up after I get home.

I've stopped buying dress shirts. I must have two dozen I've never worn and probably never will. I got them when I thought I might need them, but who needs dress shirts? Too square. If you want to make a splash with clothes you don't fool around with dress shirts.

Even before we left Woodruff, my favorite occupation other than sports and getting into fights was buying clothes. I couldn't have been beyond the fourth grade when I used to go into a store where I could charge things to my mother's account and pick up a couple of shirts or a jacket or something. Of course, she kept track of what she had bought for me, so I never got away with anything. I don't really think she minded, because she seldom got mad about it.

I've always been a clothes rebel. I remember black and pink were very big in Savannah one year. Everybody I knew—girls as well as boys—wore black-and-pink combinations. The kids would have pink sweaters and black pants or black sweaters and pink pants, that sort of thing. When I got tired of it, I added a color or two. Maybe I'd wear pink and gray one day and pink and white the next.

I wasn't exactly the St. Laurent of the sixth grade, but I noticed after a while that many of the kids changed colors when I did. I'm sure they were just as sick as I was of whatever happened to be hot at the time, but nobody would make the first move. I did because even in those days I wanted to be different.

I could be in a fight one day and setting a local clothes style the next. Believe me, the fights were more often planned than the style-setting. Like the time I started going around town in a turtleneck. Now who the hell ever thought of turtlenecks back in 1959? That was seven or eight years before they came in.

It was accidental that I happened to get my first turtleneck—in fact, a whole shipment of them reached Savannah by accident. A clerk whose son played ball with me sold me mine. I used to go into the store all the time to look at stuff, and buy something if I had the dough. Every time I went in there, I asked the guy if he had anything new.

Well, this day—it was in the fall—he said, "Kenny, we got some turtleneck shirts by mistake."

"What's a turtleneck shirt?" I said.

"Look."

He hauled out these heavy turtlenecks which weren't supposed to be in Savannah at all. Some manufacturer up north had meant to send them to the ski areas. You can't ski in Savannah because the only snow we ever get comes in flurries and melts right away. So here this guy had all these turtlenecks and he was getting ready to send them back when I walked in. I was wearing that great blue jacket I had just bought, and when I tried on a white turtleneck with it, I want to tell you, it was a real mind-bender. When I got a good look at the whole outfit—blue jacket, white turtleneck, dark-blue slacks, and white shoes—I knew it was for me.

"How much?" I asked.

"Twenty-six bucks."

"I want it," I said.

I would have wanted it if it had been a hundred and twenty-six bucks.

"Have you got twenty-six bucks?" the guy said.

"Not this minute," I said. "But I can get it. Will you save it for me?"

He not only promised to save it, he let me have it on the spot. He knew I was good for the money. All I had to do was go out and mow a few lawns or get lucky in a nine-ball pool game. It wasn't the first time I bought something from him I couldn't afford on the spot. Nor the last.

I never worried about what I could or couldn't afford. If I wanted anything badly enough I got it and found ways to pay for it later. I always managed. I earned money, or I won money at something, or if things were a little easy at home my mama helped. She knew how much I loved clothes and how important it was to me to look right.

I have to look right to be comfortable, even out on the ballfield. I suppose I'm the fussiest-dressing ballplayer in the business, but I can't help it. As long as we win, I don't care if I go 0 for 4— but, dammit, I insist on looking good going 0 for 4. Let 'em say the Hawk isn't swinging the bat, but don't ever give 'em a chance to ask who's the guy in the baggy pants striking out all the time.

I've got to have my pants so tight I can feel them against my legs. It takes me five minutes to pull them up over my calves. I roll my socks high and so tight there are deep red marks on my legs when I take the uniform off. I'll probably end up with all sorts of horrible circulation problems, but that's the way it's got to be.

That tightness around my legs and thighs gives me a feeling of strength. I don't care if the shirt's a little loose, but from the waist down I've got to feel my clothes on me. The least little blousing up of my pants bothers the hell out of me. When they're tight I feel as if I can lick the world. When there's even the sugges-

17

tion of looseness it wrecks my concentration. I can't hit the ball when I'm thinking about my pants being loose.

My demands for tightness always get me into fights with uniform makers. They think I'm nuts. Well, they may know what the dimensions of baseball pants ought to be, but they don't know the dimensions I want mine to be. I had particular trouble in Boston. Every time I was fitted for a new uniform there I had to send the pants back about four times to be altered. I even blew my stack once at Don Fitzpatrick, the Red Sox clubhouse man, who is one of the sweetest little guys I've ever known. I knew the minute I started pulling on a new pair of pants they'd be loose. They went on too easily.

"Fitzy," I yelled, "get that sonofagun in here to fix my pants. They're baggy."

Fitzy must have been having a bad day, because he yelled back, "You squawking about your pants again? Why the hell don't you just put 'em on and stop bellyaching?"

It was an easy jump from there to name-calling, and it would have been an easier one from name-calling to a fight if Fitzy were a little nearer my size. Of course, we got over it and shook hands and apologized and all that, and he ended up calling the guy in so I could give him hell personally. I was sorry afterward. I shouldn't have yelled at Fitzy. But when clothes are the issue, I'll yell at anybody.

My preference for high socks doesn't sit well with everyone I've played for. Some people demand socks be low—you know, with the pants legs way down, the way Ted Williams used to wear them when he was with the Red Sox. Charley Finley was a bug on the subject. He wanted his players wearing them low. He and I had a running argument about that all the time I was with the Athletics.

Actually, the Red Sox don't care, as long as you play ball for them. Just go out there and win a game and you can wear your socks any way you want. Manager Dick Williams is the same way. Every now and then he makes a comment, but he's never serious about it. One night last summer we were losing and I had just popped up or something. When I got back into the dugout, Dick said, "You want to wear your socks your way, you'd better start hitting again." But he smiled when he said it. Dick and I understood each other.

Like my hair. Some managers raised hell about it. Mine must have looked funny to a guy like Dick, who used to wear a crew cut, but he never once said anything about it. There's really no reason for anybody to. It's long, but it's neat. One of the Boston baseball writers said I'm the only guy he ever knew who came out of the barber's with longer hair than when he went in.

During spring training at Winter Haven I developed a thing for mustaches. Since I can't grow my own, I went out and bought one for eight bucks. Bill Crowley, the Red Sox publicity director, offered me eight bucks not to wear it. I told him to keep his money.

I'm young enough to get a kick out of everything, including moppy hair, crazy clothes, and false mustaches. I don't care what's in or out of style. Why, Nehrus went out last spring, but they're not out for me. I'll wear them as long as they look right on me. I'll wear anything that looks right on me.

Let's face it—I'm a guy in love with myself. Why, I even pasted a picture of myself over my locker in the Red Sox clubhouse at Winter Haven last spring. When Joe Garagiola asked me why, I said it was because I'm my favorite ballplayer.

"Great guy," Joe said, "but he's got to come out of his shell."

Well, I'm trying. That's really why I look in the mirror every day, flash myself a brilliant smile, and, nose or no nose, say, "You handsome sonofagun, don't you ever die!"

2 | Football and Nine-Ball

Crazy things are always happening to me. They've been happening all my life, which began in 1941 in the little South Carolina mill town of Woodruff. We were pretty well off and lived in a nice big house. My father owned two bakeries, one in Woodruff, the other in Spartanburg, about twenty miles to the north. He and my mama were divorced when I was twelve, after we moved to Savannah, and I have rarely seen him since. I have a sister, Iris, who's six years older than I am.

My best friend was Johnny Crocker, whose father was our mailman. My first girl was Tina Smith, whose brother Don was another of my pals. I couldn't have been more than five years old then, but I still remember Tina. The trouble was, she couldn't, or wouldn't, do the things we did—like fighting or playing ball or going skinny-dipping in the swimming hole—so it wasn't much of a romance. Anyhow, she was a year younger than I, so we didn't have a hell of a lot in common. Yet whenever I think back to all the girls I ever knew, she is the first one who pops into my mind.

But she didn't teach me anything. The one I really learned from was a very pretty girl named Anne something. She was a couple of years older—in the sixth grade, I think, when I was in the fourth—and one day she and I were playing in a cemetery. Finally, we sat on top of a tombstone and she said she was going to kiss me. That was the first time I ever was really kissed by a girl, and, man, I'll never forget it. Anne was only about ten.

That started a big romance that lasted until she insisted on going out with her brother and me when we went hunting one day. Told me she wanted to see if I was a good enough hunter to provide for her after we got married. While we were out, she grabbed my rifle and wouldn't give it back. I didn't like her any more after that. What a dope I was! Today I sure wouldn't get into a fight over a rifle with a girl as pretty as Anne.

Johnny Crocker and I once sold the birds we shot for a penny apiece, then bought a pack of cigarettes when we had twenty cents. That's what they cost then. I was six years old when I smoked for the first time. It made me sick and I never smoked again until I grew up.

One of my most vivid memories of Woodruff is my close friendship with some colored kids who lived four or five hundred feet from our house. I used to go with them to a deep gully half a mile away, where you could swing off a vine and drop fifty feet into the water if you hit it right. If you didn't, you'd slide down a bank of brambles and get scratched from head to foot. Many a night I came home all carved up from those brambles.

Maybe it seems odd that a white kid like me in the Deep South would have many colored friends, but Woodruff was that kind of town. It really didn't have a colored section that I was aware of, although the schools were segregated. Colored people lived all over town, and I played and fought with their kids just the way I did with white kids. As a result, I am one Southerner who grew up without prejudices at all.

Football, basketball, and swimming were my favorite sports, and I don't mind telling you I was good at all three. One afternoon

I learned the hard way how to swim fast. Mr. Crocker used to take us to a place called Wareshoals—it wasn't a town, just part of a river. Down a little way from where we were was a vine hanging off a tree where you could swing out over the water, like the spot near where I lived, but Mr. Crocker wouldn't let us near it. He always warned us to stick to one spot, where it was safe and not too deep.

One day I waited until he was in the water and I was out, then I ran over to that vine, swung out over the water, and dropped. As I approached the surface of the river I saw half a dozen water moccasins—big, long, ugly snakes—right on top of the water. I surfaced swimming like mad. I must have broken all Woodruff speed records getting the hell away from there. Mr. Crocker was waiting for me on the bank and he beat my rear half off. I remember thinking snake bites couldn't have been worse than that.

He saved my life once at Wareshoals. I wandered about fifty yards over from where we were supposed to stay to where there was a big rock high over the water that looked good to dive off. I went headfirst and got stuck in the mud. If Mr. Crocker hadn't noticed my feet straight up and the rest of me out of sight, there never would have been a Hawk Harrelson. I was pretty nearly suffocated by the time he hauled me out.

It was just about that time—I know I wasn't more than five —that I had my own .22 rifle. I used to hunt wild turkey by myself over near my grandparents' farm. If you've never lived in the country, that might sound funny, but it wasn't at all unusual. One of the first things a country kid learned was how to handle a gun.

I was a good shot, but I didn't know one bird from another. I went out from my grandma's one time and killed about eight birds. I had so many, they were sticking out of pockets and dragging on the ground behind me when I got home, proud as could be.

"Look, Grandma," I called, "I got me some wild turkeys."

"Wild turkeys, my foot," she yelled, "those are my guineas."

Man, I got hell for that. My fanny was red for days.

HAWK

My daddy taught me how to drive a car when I was six. I used to sit in his lap and do everything but use the clutch, brake, and accelerator, which I was too small to reach. But I did all the steering and hand shifting—he never touched the wheel. He made an automobile nut out of me. I always loved cars so much that I did some racing when I was older.

The first time I ever played baseball was on the dirt road leading up to my grandparents' farmhouse. I just sort of tagged along with my cousins, Francis, Travis, and Buford Johnson. They were all bigger, but they got a kick out of seeing me catch and throw the ball. I was a better fielder then than I am now.

Although my dad didn't work in the mill, he played ball for the Woodruff mill team. He was a little guy and batted cross-handed. Woodruff was in a semipro league that played surrounding towns. My father played right field and, small as he was, could hit the hell out of the ball. He taught me to bat cross-handed, and I never learned it was wrong until I played Little League ball in Savannah.

One of the last things I remember about Woodruff was playing ball in a big cow pasture that sloped sharply up from the infield. If you hit the ball over the hill it was an automatic home run because the outfielders wouldn't chase it. The guy who hit it had to go after it. That was when I first knew I could be a good hitter. Even batting cross-handed, I was up and down that hill all afternoon chasing my own home runs.

I guess I might have grown up in Woodruff, but my dad's bakery there burned down. Then he sold the one in Spartanburg and went to work for a guy he knew who ran a bakery in Charlotte. We were there only a few months when he got a job in an atomic-energy plant in Barnwell, South Carolina. That was when we moved to Savannah. It was a hundred-mile commute to Barnwell, but my dad made it every day until he and my mama separated. Then he went back to South Carolina and we stayed in Savannah.

24

Football and Nine-Ball

I grew up in Savannah like the little girl with the little curl in the middle of her forehead. When I was good I was very, very good and when I was bad I was horrid. Believe me, one minute I'd do something so nice people would point me out as the kind of son or brother they'd like to have. The next I'd be in such a foolish jam from a fight or something that parents would look the other way and say, "Thank God he isn't mine."

School didn't mean anything but sports to me. I was forever playing hooky, at first just for the hell of it and later either to play pool or golf. I got promoted from grade to grade because any teacher who had me once had had it. In justice to myself, I will say I wasn't a dope. I was bright enough to do whatever classroom work had to be done. I just didn't get around to doing it very often.

Good, bad, or indifferent, I had a few things going for me. I liked people and they liked me, so I was a popular kid. I figured then—as I do now—that it's just as easy to be nice as to be nasty and a hell of a lot more fun. I know it's the most immodest thing in the world to say, but I was the best all-round schoolboy athlete in Savannah. I could do anything. All it ever took was a little practice. I was a stickout in such conventional sports as football, basketball, and baseball, and such unconventional ones as pool, arm-wrestling, auto racing, fighting, and blackjack.

I didn't discover golf until my junior year in high school. From then on, no matter what I played because I was expected to, golf was the only game I *wanted* to play and it was just about all I *did* play practically my whole junior year.

I was always getting into trouble, but I had fundamentally decent instincts. I worked as hard as I played and gave my mama money whenever I made any. She earned fifty-five dollars a week as a secretary, and she could do more with that than most people could do with half again as much.

We lived in a poor section of town, but our house was always neat and well kept, and we had nice things in it. I didn't have the

most expensive clothes in the world, but I never walked out looking like a slob, although sometimes I came back a bloody, ragged
mess from a fight.

Yet my mama always seemed to understand. Even after a fight
or a bad report card or a visit from the truant officer or when I
came home late after playing pool three-quarters of the night,
she'd say through her tears, "Kenny, I *know* you're a good boy.
But I wish you wouldn't do things like this."

And I'd put my arm around her and say, "Mama, don't you
worry. Someday I'm going to make a lot of money and I'll buy
you a Cadillac."

I remember more of the bad things than the good, but there
was one good thing I'll never forget. When I walked to school,
I practiced bouncing a football until I could hit it on the tip so it
would come right back to me every time. One morning a little kid
was standing at the curb across the street absolutely petrified—
frozen to one spot and just screaming. I walked over, and there
was a coral snake about ten inches long lying in the gutter. I
pushed the kid away and bounced the tip of the football off the
snake's head until he was dead, then walked the kid home.

It was probably the only time in my whole school career that
I had a legitimate excuse for being late.

My temper, always quick, was shortest whenever somebody
laughed at the way I looked or talked. One day before my sister,
Iris, got married, I had to wear a pair of her dungarees to school
because mine were either dirty or still wet on the line after an all-
night rain. Girls' dungarees zip up the side instead of the middle,
and I was so afraid somebody would notice that I kept my shirttails
out to hide the zipper. But when we were playing basketball at
recess and I jumped to make a shot, my shirttails went up and one
of the other boys saw the zipper.

"Kenny's wearing girls' dungarees," he yelled, and when he
started laughing I went after him. I just beat his brains out, I was

so mad. The next day I saw him picking on a little kid, and went after him again. That time he beat my brains out.

I could play football, basketball, and baseball so well that all the junior high schools in Savannah wanted me and the high schools were waiting for me to grow up. I must have been the only grammar-school kid in the country to be recruited to junior high, and I guess maybe the only junior-high-school kid to be recruited to high school.

When I was in the seventh grade at Eli Whitney Grammar School, the coaches of every one of the city's four junior highs came to talk to my mama about my going to their schools. We decided on Chatham because I liked the coach best, but the next year I switched to Richard Arnold because they made us a better offer. In return for my going there, they put a gas heater in the house and supplied us with free gas all year.

I was the regular quarterback two years. When I reached the ninth grade, we beat the hell out of Chatham and went on to win the city football championship. After winning all our nine regular games, we went over to Brunswick to play Glen Academy's junior varsity in the first of two postseason games. I was running a rollout in the third period when a Glen Academy lineman broke through and belted my leg so hard he knocked me right out of the ball game, which we eventually lost.

We didn't practice the next day, and the day after I had a terrible charley horse. The coach told me to put on a uniform, but I said, "I can't practice. Look—I can't even walk."

"Put on the uniform," he said.

"You know how I love to play," I said. "I'd practice if I could."

"Either you put on the uniform or you turn it in," he said.

I thought he was kidding, but he wasn't. He actually kicked me off the club. I was so sore I swore I'd never play anything for Richard Arnold again, and I never did.

In the meantime, the high-school coaches were coming around

to get me. Commercial High was in the same building as Richard Arnold—they had split sessions—and the Commercial coach was a wonderful guy named M. A. Spellman. He wanted me to go there, but so did the coach at Savannah, the biggest high school in the state. And R. C. Haupt, who owned the Coastal Butane Gas Company and whose son, Bubba, was one of my best friends, wanted me to go to Benedictine, a Catholic military school. Mr. Haupt was so eager for me to go there that he offered to pay for my tuition, books, uniform, everything.

Of course I had to finish the ninth grade at Richard Arnold before I could go anywhere. I was still there when Mr. Spellman came over to me one day and said, "Kenny, you come to Commercial and be my quarterback."

"I haven't made up my mind yet," I said.

"Well," said Mr. Spellman, "while you're deciding, you can play in the Blue-Gold game."

To play in Commercial's Blue-Gold game was a big honor. Usually, only juniors and seniors were in it because it was an annual spring football fixture for the older boys. An occasional sophomore made it, but never before had a junior-high-school kid been chosen.

So when spring came around, there I was going to one school and playing football for another. The Blue-Gold game, which attracted not only the student body and alumni of Commercial but football fans from all over Savannah, was played at night at Coke Field. We were supposed to meet at the school, on the corner of Anderson and Thirty-fifth Streets, at six o'clock. We would dress there and go to the field by bus for the game at eight.

I was so anxious to be on time that I started hitchhiking from home at four o'clock. The very first guy who came along picked me up and fifteen minutes later dropped me off in front of the school. With an hour and three-quarters to kill and not a soul around to talk to, I decided to go over and shoot a little nine-ball. There was a poolroom at Anderson and Thirty-first, only four blocks away, so I could make it back in a couple of minutes.

I had two or three bucks, which I figured to lose fast or run up into a little bundle. A guy about forty-five was looking for a game when I walked in, but it took me a few minutes to get him to play me.

"You're just a kid," he said. "I don't want to take your money."

"Maybe you won't," I said.

"Have you got any?"

"Enough," I said. "How about half-a-buck nine-ball?"

The guy looked around, shrugged, and said, "O.K. But don't lose any more than you have. It's got to be strictly cash."

"O.K.," I said. "The only thing is, I have to quit at five minutes to six—win, lose, or draw."

He agreed, and we started. Nine-ball is the fastest game in pool, with the first guy having a big advantage because he gets everything that goes in on the break. If he can run in the rest of the balls in their proper order he can win before his opponent gets a chance to shoot.

Now, here's this grown man playing a ninth-grade kid, and you couldn't blame him for being confident. He acted very patronizing until I ran the first game after getting the break. I was feeling good, and the next thing I knew I couldn't do anything wrong. I kept winning, winning, winning, and at half a buck a game I went five, ten, fifteen, twenty, twenty-five bucks in front. At six o'clock I was still hot, so I said to myself, "The hell with this. I'm going to keep playing. I can make it to the game all right." By six thirty we had split a couple of games and I was still twenty-five ahead.

"I have to leave," I said.

"You can't quit now," the guy said. "You've got twenty-five bucks of my money."

"I told you I'd play until six," I said. "I'm half an hour late now, but I'll give you a chance to get your money back all at once. How about one game for twenty-five bucks?"

He agreed. I broke the rack, ran out the game before he could put his cue on the table, grabbed his fifty bucks, and ran the four blocks back to the school. The bus had left already, but Johnny, the equipment man, who was slow-witted and a little tongue-tied, was still there, scared to death.

"Coach is awful mad at you," he stammered, as I ripped off my clothes. "I kept telling him you'd get here, but the bus went anyhow."

I left all my stuff in a heap on the floor, put everything on but my shoes, followed Johnny out the door, and he drove me to the field. When I got there a little after seven, Mr. Spellman yelled, "Kenny, I've got half a mind not to play you. Where in the world were you?"

"Coach," I said, "I couldn't get a ride. I was thumbing over from home and nobody would pick me up."

It was probably the only excuse he would have accepted.

"All right, Kenny," he said. "You're the Blue quarterback. And since you're the youngest boy on the field, you can have Billy Phillips for one of your ends."

Billy Phillips, who stood about six feet five, had led the state schoolboys in pass receiving the previous fall. Having him was like getting two touchdowns handed to you.

Well, we killed that Gold club—absolutely killed it. I threw two touchdown passes to Billy, a couple more to other guys, and we won big. When it was over, Mr. Spellman said, "Kenny, you're only going to be a sophomore, but I'll guarantee you're my first-string quarterback next year."

"I'll be here," I said—and I really thought I would be.

I sure felt great—until I got back to the high-school locker room. My clothes were still in a heap on the floor, but somebody had taken the fifty bucks out of the pants pocket.

The next day our house was crawling with coaches—every high school in the city except Commercial was represented. I kept telling my mama I wanted Commercial because the coach was such a wonderful guy, but all the other coaches brought up something we had never even thought of. Commercial wasn't an accredited high school. Even if you graduated from there at the head of the class you still wouldn't have enough credits for college.

I thought the Savannah High coach came close to getting me. He sat with the two of us and said, "Mrs. Harrelson, I want to tell you something. I've been coaching for twenty-five years and this is the first time I've ever gone to anybody's home to get a boy to come to our school. That's how badly I want Kenny. And you know he'd be best off at Savannah, because it's the biggest and best in town."

But my mama had already made up her mind, and nobody could change it. She wanted me to go to Benedictine. Not only had Mr. Haupt promised to pay all the bills, but it was a military school with tight discipline. For that reason alone, I didn't want any part of the place. All my life I had heard how rough it was. The upperclassmen kicked hell out of freshmen and newly arrived sophomores, hazing them, making them run errands, and pushing them around. I couldn't take that. I'd have nothing but fights.

That didn't make any difference to my mama. When Vic Mell, the Benedictine coach, came over that evening with Mr. Haupt, she told them that was where I was going.

So that night, instead of going to bed looking forward to three easy years at Commercial, I couldn't sleep worrying about being hazed, harassed, jugged and piling up demerits under a tough pseudomilitary system. I knew guys at Benedictine who had gone through it. As freshmen they had their asses paddled off for the least little thing. And all through school, they were subject to a fate worse than death—walking the jug if you got five demerits. Walking the jug was marching up and down a concrete courtyard for three hours after school, with an M-1 rifle on your shoulder. I could see myself doing it every day because I just knew I'd break all known records for demerits.

On top of that, I was an entering sophomore, which meant I'd be subject to all the crap upperclassmen handed out to freshmen. I'd be in a fight a day.

At least there was one compensation—the Benedictine kids always looked like a million bucks. They went around wearing the best-looking uniforms in town.

3 | Fun, Games, and Trouble

I got into all the trouble I anticipated at Benedictine, because I averaged about fifteen demerits a week, but sports saved me from walking the jug anywhere near as much as I expected. We had drill until four o'clock on Tuesday and Thursdays, so you could walk the jug only Mondays, Wednesdays, and Fridays. I had enough demerits to pull the jug by my first Wednesday in school, but I got out of it ridiculously easily. I just went up to Coach Vic Mell and said, "I can't practice this afternoon. I have to walk the jug."

"I'll take care of that," he said.

From then on, I was set. The coach insisted he had to have his sophomore quarterback at every practice, so I didn't have to walk the jug much all fall. Benedictine had had a hell of a season the year before—won eight out of nine or something like that—and any football player was a big man on the campus. The upper-classmen didn't give me more than a token hazing, and few guys ever gave me the jug.

As soon as football ended, we went right into basketball, and the basketball coach was as fussy about my showing up for practice as the football coach had been. Because he had four seniors and a junior, he didn't start me at first. But one of the seniors was hurt in an early game, and I broke into the starting lineup in a game against Glen Academy at Brunswick.

Brunswick is about eighty miles from Savannah. We went down there by bus, along with the press and our cheerleaders, a group of kids from St. Vincent's, a Catholic girls' school which supplied the cheerleaders for all our sports teams. Glen Academy had a real strong club that was supposed to beat our brains out, but the Hawk saved the night. I played one of the best games I can remember—pumped in thirty-three points, did a hell of a job on defense, was a real hot dog—and we murdered Glen.

Remember, I was only a sophomore and had already had a great football season, so I wasn't exactly a shrinking violet, especially after that game. I swaggered back onto the bus, went way in back, and sat right in the middle of the last row of seats, where I could see the whole aisle and the whole aisle could see me. I knew what I was doing—the girls always stood in the aisle leading cheers when we traveled, and I didn't want any of them to miss me.

Facing me halfway down was a cute little one, and when I smiled at her she smiled back. Then I winked and she winked, and all the way up to Savannah, the two of us smiled and winked at each other without exchanging a word. I didn't even get a chance to talk to her when we arrived home because she was gone by the time I got out of the bus. The whole team was going to a party at Dickie Buttimer's house that night, and I hoped maybe she'd be there. Sure enough, she was.

Her name was Betty Ann Pacifici, and she was going steady with a guy named Bubsy Ryan, who's now the District Attorney of Savannah. Much more important to me at the time was the fact that he was my company commander, the guy who gave out demerits for drill infractions. Campus hero or no campus hero, I was still just a buck private, with a big collection of demerits already slapped on by this guy. When I arrived at the party, he and Betty Ann were in a hell of an argument, and I didn't have to hear a word to know what it was about because Bubsy kept looking in my direction. Suddenly he turned around and walked out, while Betty Ann stayed. I went right over, and in two minutes we were old friends.

Long before the party was over, at least half a dozen guys told me, "Man, you're in trouble. This is Bubsy's girl. He'll give you so many demerits you'll be walking the jug for the rest of the year."

I overslept the next morning and just made it to school in time for eight-fifteen inspection. When Bubsy reached me, he looked me up and down and said, "Why are your shoes dirty?"

"I got up late this morning and didn't have a chance to shine them."

"Why didn't you shine them before you went to bed last night?"

"We had the ball game in Brunswick and then the party," I said. "By the time I got home I was too tired to do anything but go to bed."

"Your brass is filthy," Bubsy said.

"I didn't have time to shine that either," I said.

"You need a shave."

"I don't have much of a beard anyhow," I said.

"And your pants aren't pressed."

I waited for the blow to fall. How many demerits? How many hours walking the jug? Can the coach get me out of it this time?

Bubsy looked me up and down again, then said, "Well, I'll let you off because we won last night and you played a good game. But that's the only reason. Next time you'll get it good."

He might have added, "Stay away from my girl," but that wouldn't have mattered, because Betty Ann broke up with him and started going with me the next day. Although we spent practically all our time fighting and making up, we got married before I was out of Benedictine, when we were both seventeen.

We've been fighting and making up, fighting and making up ever since. We have four kids now and a house in the Boston suburb of Lynnfield, and we're still fighting. That's why she's in the house and I'm in an apartment in town. I'd like to make up because I still love her, but, as these lines are written, she isn't having any. Maybe ten or twelve years with the Hawk is about all any girl can take, but I still have hopes.

One of our fights when we started going together led me into a terrible jam. My sister had a new Studebaker Hawk, which could go like hell, and I was always pestering her to let me drive it. One night she let me use it to go down to Savannah Beach to see Betty Ann, who was living there then. We went somewhere for ice cream or something and on the way home got into an awful argument. When I pulled up in front of her house she was so mad she jumped out of the car without kissing me goodnight and ran.

Just as mad as she was, I stepped on the gas and zoomed off. When I reached the highway to Savannah, I met a guy from Benedictine named Buddy something, driving a brand new Chevy.

"Hey Kenny," he yelled. "You want to race?"

"Hell, yes," I yelled back.

We knew the highway was heavily patrolled, but I was so sore at Betty Ann I didn't give a damn. Buddy and I lined up, and off we went. His Chevy was fast, but Iris's little Studebaker was faster. We were on a four-mile stretch of straight road—not a curve in it— and pretty soon I had that car up to a hundred miles an hour. Suddenly we went by the little red devil, that revolving red light on top of a police car, parked at a corner waiting for a couple of pigeons like us.

When he came roaring after us, I looked in the rearview mirror and saw Buddy turn off to the right, so I took the first left I could, pulled off the road, put out the lights and swung the car around behind a huge clump of sagebrush, right on the sand. After about ten minutes, I figured I was all right, but just as I reached the highway, along came that little red devil again. This big cop pulled up beside me, got out, reached into my car and hauled me out.

Still mad at Betty Ann, I had only one person to take it out on—the cop. He had grabbed me real hard anyhow, so I swung on him. He didn't have to hit me back for me to know I was in trouble. He just bundled me into the police car, took me to the station, told me I was going into jail and that I could make one phone call.

It was two-thirty in the morning, and the last person in the world I'd call was my mama. I decided to phone a lawyer whom I didn't know very well but who went to a lot of our games and was always telling me what a great athlete I was.

"This is Kenny Harrelson," I said. "I'm in jail. Can you come down and get me out?"

"Kenny Harrelson," he said, "if you're stupid enough to get yourself put into jail at this hour, you can stay there. I'm not going to do anything to get you out." Then he hung up.

There went my one phone call. As the cop led me to my cell, I thought of dozens of people I might have called—Mr. Haupt, Mr. Pacifici, one of the neighbors, the father of any one of my close friends, even Coach Mell—but by then it was too late. As they were putting me into the cell, they were letting out a guy who lived a block and a half from me. I didn't know him, but he knew who I was.

"I'm going right home," he said. "Do you want me to tell your mother?"

"No, no, not my mother," I said. "Anybody but her."

After he left, I looked around the filthy cell, which smelled of vomit and urine and everything else horrible you can think of. It was the first time I'd ever been in jail, and I couldn't imagine anything worse. The only things in the room were a messy toilet, a bucket, and a cot with a thin, stained mattress. I sat down on it, put my head in my hands, and cried.

Cheez, you dumb bastard, I thought. *You break up with your girl, you get into a race in your sister's car, you run it up to a*

37

hundred miles an hour, you punch a cop, you land in jail, you use up your one phone call on a guy who turns out to be a louse, and now what the hell are you going to do?

I was still sitting there, weeping, mad and sorry for myself, when the cop came back, opened the cell door and said, "You're the luckiest kid in town. Your friend's father is the mayor of Savannah Beach. He phoned and told us to let you out. Come on, I'll take you back to your car."

I didn't know Buddy's old man was the mayor. Hell, I didn't even know Buddy's last name. I don't know it to this day.

Some of the fights I got into were over Betty. One night we were standing in front of her house after walking home from a beach party when three guys drove by. One yelled out something nasty, and I called him a dirty name. When the guy stopped and backed up, I told Betty Ann to go into the house. I was sixteen, a big, brave hero, but when the driver, a mean-looking guy, said, "You know, I ought to kill you," the big, brave hero suddenly became a scared little coward. There was no way I could lick this guy, let alone his friends. The last thing I wanted was a fight—not then. All I could do was try to stall him.

"You know Bubba Noonan?" I said.

Bubba Noonan, the toughest kid in town, was like Rocky Marciano—he had never lost a fight. He liked me because I was a good athlete, and he went around the same places I did. There was one teen-age hangout called the Triple X, and I couldn't remember a night that I didn't see Bubba there.

"Yeah, I know Bubba Noonan," the guy said.

"Well," I said, "if you want a fight, you take your two friends over to the Triple X tomorrow night and Bubba and I will beat your asses off."

The next night I couldn't find Bubba at the Triple X. I'll bet he was there almost every other night of his life, but this time he didn't show up. I stood there and thought, *Good Gawd Almighty, you've gone and done it again.* If those guys came around before Bubba did, I was a dead duck.

Sure enough, the three of them walked in, and the big guy said, "Where's your boy?"

"He's not here," I said.

"You probably don't even know him," the guy said. "We're all ready to go. Are you?"

"I can't take on the three of you," I said.

"You don't have to," he said. "I'll fight you alone."

I didn't want to fight him alone either, but with all those kids around I couldn't get out of it. I guess just about everybody in the joint followed us out to a place behind the parking lot, and we went at it. Believe me, it wasn't much of a fight. This big slob knocked me off my feet with one punch, and every time I got up he knocked me down again. I finally realized it was stupid to keep going, so I stayed down and that was the end of that.

I blamed it all on Bubba Noonan for picking that one night not to show up at the Triple X. I never liked him much after that.

When the Benedictine basketball season ended, it was time for spring training. Every year the football team spent two weeks working out at the Marine base on Parris Island. On the way over in the bus I played blackjack with a kid named Billy, who had been on the Richard Arnold football team with me. He was as crazy as I was, always getting into foolish arguments and fights over nothing.

We started at a nickel a hand, then went up to a dime, then a quarter. We were just about even when we arrived at Parris Island, so we decided to play one hand for a buck. While the other kids were piling out of the bus, we were playing that last big hand. I won it, but Billy grabbed the money and ran.

"Give me the dough," I yelled. "I won it."

"The hell you did," he said. "*I* won it."

His suitcase was on the rack over our heads, so I hauled it down, opened it, and took half a dozen pairs of his socks.

"O.K.," I said. "You keep the money. I'll keep the socks."

By this time we were near the door, the last kids off the bus, and Billy yelled, "Gimme my socks."

"Gimme my money," I yelled back.

Now we were off the bus, standing in a driving rainstorm, yelling like hell as we moved toward each other.

"Billy," I said, "you take one more step and I'm going to drill you."

He took another step, and I let him have it—bam!—right in the chops, and my hand hurt so much I started yelling. Billy, a wild man when he was mad, lashed out with a punch that I saw coming all the way, but I was thinking about my hand and just froze. His punch landed squarely on my nose, and *that* hurt so much the tears started streaming down my face.

By this time, about a dozen Marines were standing there watching what had developed into a pretty good little fight. I could hear them yelling, some for Billy, some for me, as the two of us whaled away at each other. Some of the Benedictine boys who had missed us finally came back and broke it up, but by then Billy and I had just about killed each other.

There was blood all over the place from cuts and bruises as the fight had progressed, but we had both done the most damage with our first punches. Mine had broken both my hand and Billy's jaw. His had broken my nose—for the third time. Neither of us dared to say anything to the coach. We knew he'd be mad enough at us just for fighting. When he found out what we had done to each other he'd blow his stack.

But that first night at Parris Island he didn't say anything to either of us. My hand hurt and my nose hurt, and Billy couldn't eat and had trouble talking, but the coach acted as if nothing had happened. We both stayed as far away from him as we could. He didn't say a word for the first few days, when we worked mostly on calisthenics and running and all that stuff to get into shape. One day he divided us up into small groups, and, as the quarterback, I had to take snaps from the center.

The first time I touched the ball my whole right arm felt as if somebody had put a match to it, and I had to bite my lips to keep from yelling. By the third or fourth snap I couldn't stand it any longer.

"Coach," I said, "there's something the matter with my hand."

"Let me look at it," he said.

As he reached out to touch it I flinched and said, "It's killing me. I don't know what it is."

He felt around, then said, "I think it's broken." He got a couple of those wooden tongue depressors from a first-aid kit and made a splint out of them.

"Go out and just do handoffs," he said. "And after practice we'll go into Beaufort and see a doctor."

Beaufort is only a few miles from Parris Island, but it seemed like a hundred. Coach Mell ate my ass out all the way.

"What's the matter with you, Kenny?" he said. "With you at quarterback, we'd have the best team in the state. So what happens? You get into a silly fight, break your hand, and now you can't pass."

"Well, it's only spring," I said.

"You'll miss the rest of spring practice," Mell said. "And most of baseball, too. You won't be able to play that for weeks."

I mumbled something about being all right for baseball, but he paid no attention. He just kept yakking and yakking while I prayed we'd hurry up and get to where we were going. He was still bawling me out when we pulled up in front of the doctor's at Beaufort.

The doctor didn't like the looks of my hand at all. After taking X rays, he said it wasn't healing properly, so the coach decided to send me back to Savannah to see our own doctor, a nice old guy named Edwards. By the time I walked into his office the next day he had already seen the X rays. After he looked at my hand he said, "I'm sorry, son. I'm going to have to break it and reset it."

"The hell you will," I said, and got up to leave.

"Sit down," he snapped. "What do you want, a deformed hand? Then you won't be able to play anything."

"Well, can't you fix it some other way?" I said.

"Now, don't be a baby. I'll give you some novocain and you won't feel a thing."

So he gave me a shot of novocain, then took my wrist in one hand and my thumb and forefinger in the other, and said, "This is going to hurt just a little."

"Hey, wait," I yelled. "Give the Novocain a chance to . . . Yeow!!!"

When he yanked, I jumped right off the chair and the tears started rolling down my cheeks. As I yelled and cried and cursed, the old doc grinned and said, "Oh, come on, it didn't hurt that much. Anyhow, it's all over."

"You still have to set it, don't you?"

"That's what the novocain was for," he said. "Now you *really* won't feel anything."

I walked out with a cast on my hand, and it didn't come off for six weeks. In the meantime, about the only thing I could play was miniature golf. At that time, I still thought golf was a stupid game, but I liked to bat my way around those little putting courses. Savannah had a dozen of them, and even when I was a kid I was a champion. I held the national record for juniors, 27 for eighteen holes—nine one-putt and nine two-putt holes. For all I know, I still hold it. Par was 36, and I broke that regularly.

Every year they had a city-wide tournament for juniors and seniors, with the champions of each division playing each other. Cast and all, I won the junior division, for which I got an English racer bike and a hundred-and-fifty-dollar gift certificate at a hardware store. The grand prize was the use of a Mercury for two weeks, plus a two-week vacation for two people in Florida.

Well, in the finals I played a guy named Earl Fritz, the senior champion, who had been the best miniature golfer in Savannah for years. We played eighteen holes to a standoff, so we had to go extra holes, sudden death. We both aced the first one, but the second was real tough. I putted first, barely missed acing it, and Earl won when his shot dropped in. I rode the bike home and gave the gift certificate to my mama, who used it for screens and other stuff she needed for the house.

My hand was getting better, and I was looking forward to playing the last few games of the baseball season for Benedictine. But about three days before I went to have the cast taken off, I ruined any chance of that while breaking up with Betty Ann for about the fiftieth time. We got into this terrible argument over the phone —I don't even remember what it was about. When I slammed down the receiver, I was so mad I threw the phone book up in the air, and it hit me in the eye coming down. I couldn't see, and it hurt so much I went to the doctor. He found I had torn something or other, and I had to wear a patch for the next four weeks.

Betty Ann and I made up the next day, and all the time I wore the patch we didn't have one fight. But I blew the rest of the Benedictine baseball season, which set me up great with Vic Mell. He coached baseball, too.

I never played very much high-school baseball because there always seemed to be something in the way. One year it was my broken hand. The next it was golf. I think my senior year was the only one in which I played an entire season. But from the time I was ten or eleven I had always played baseball with one team or another. I went right up the line—Little League, Babe Ruth League, and American Legion Junior League. Because I had a good arm and was always big and strong for my age, I pitched as well as played the infield and outfield. I never got much early coaching but learned mostly from observation.

For example, you remember I used to imitate my father and bat cross-handed as a little kid in Woodruff. Nobody told me it was wrong, either there or when I first began playing Little League in Savannah. But by then I had noticed from watching other kids that I had the wrong hand on top—the left as I batted right-handed—so I shifted myself.

It would have been very easy for me to become a switch hitter, because a kid hitting cross-handed stands at the plate right-handed and holds his hands like a lefty. Perhaps a professional coach would have encouraged me, but it might not have occurred to a Little League coach. And it certainly didn't occur to me. I was comfortable on the right side of the plate, so I never even tried to change.

I don't remember when I started catching the ball with one hand—it might have been after I broke my hand in that fight at Parris Island. In any event, none of my coaches, either in Savannah or in organized baseball, could get me to use two hands. I played mostly the outfield in high school and came into organized baseball as an outfielder. Even as a seventeen-year-old Class D ballplayer at Olean in the New York–Penn League, I caught the ball one-handed. And I still do it in the big leagues, whether I play first base or the outfield. People have heart failure watching me, but I generally manage to make the play.

Although I've always liked baseball, it never was my favorite sport. I wasn't one of those kids so dedicated that I aimed for the big leagues from the start. As a matter of fact, I didn't take the game seriously until the summer following my junior year in high school. That was the year we won the state Junior Legion championship. We had a great club—Post 135—and scouts followed us wherever we played.

Baseball scouts can't recruit kids until their high-school class graduates, but there's no law against talking to them or getting friendly with their families before then. Guys representing one team or another, were always coming to us, but I don't know many of them by name. I wasn't even sure I wanted to play baseball for a living. It really was my worst sport. At that time, basketball was my best, unless you counted pool and arm-wrestling, at which I was a stickout. And in 1957 I was a better football than baseball player. I also had some ideas about auto racing. I won a few drag races, and it looked as if that might be a pretty good way to make a buck.

That was all before I fell in love with golf. As a caddie, I thought the game was a waste of time, but I got hooked on it the first time I played a full round, and I've been hooked ever since.

The more I look back on it, the odder it seems that it took me so long. I started caddying at eleven or twelve as one of a dozen ways of picking up some dough. For me, it was like shining shoes, or collecting milk bottles to turn in for nickels, or cutting grass— a way of making money. Outside of miniature golf, which was just putting, I had never swung a club until just before I turned sixteen.

Eventually, I became one hell of a good golfer. In the groove, I could break par consistently, and often get down into the 60s. Most guys who play that well grew up on golf courses, usually as caddies who played every chance they got. But as a kid, I never spent one minute more than I had to on a course. I carried a guy's clubs around, and unless he wanted to go more than eighteen holes, I collected my money and went off to do something else when the round was over.

I thought all golfers were nuts. I used to watch these guys get tense and mad at themselves and talk about grips and stances and swings and wonder what the hell was wrong with them.

Well, one day in August, after we won that 1957 Junior Legion state championship, our coach, an Air Force officer named Floyd

45

Doss, invited three of us to go out and play a round of golf with him. I didn't think much of the idea, but I admired Floyd so much I figured anything he liked couldn't be all bad. Somebody lent me a set of clubs, Floyd told me which ones to use, and I birdied the first hole. It took me 118 strokes to get around the whole course, but by the time I finished, I was a gone goose.

I couldn't get home fast enough to tell my mama I had to have a set of golf clubs. Between what she could scrape up and what I could earn or win I had enough for a whole set of woods and irons before the week was over. From then on I spent more time on the Mary Calder golf course than anywhere else in Savannah.

School started, and I didn't go near the football field—too busy playing golf. Coach Vic Mell kept after me until I finally went out just to please him. I practiced for about a week, until I broke my nose that time the bar broke. That was enough for me. I remember thinking on the way home, *This is not my game. This is somebody else's action, but not mine.*

The coach was so upset he came over to the house one night to see if he could talk my mama into getting me to come back.

"Mrs. Harrelson," he said, "you've got to talk to him. He's the greatest quarterback I've ever seen—absolutely the finest quarterback in the whole state of Georgia. You've just got to talk him into playing. He can get a college education from football and then be a pro star."

But I didn't want any part of it, and my mama agreed. She hadn't wanted me to play football in the first place, so she wasn't about to try to push me back into the game. Of course, if I could have foreseen those half-million-dollar contracts good quarterbacks get today maybe I'd have felt differently. But I was a few years ahead of my time. I never played football again.

It didn't matter to my mama. She wouldn't go across the street to watch me play football, but she traveled miles for basketball and baseball games I played. I remember her driving all the way across the state for an American Legion baseball tournament in Columbus—commuted the whole way four days in a row. Columbus is maybe two hundred miles from Savannah. My mama would get off work at four in the afternoon and be at the ball park in time for the first or second inning by eight, then she'd spend half the night driving home. That was the year we won the championship.

She rarely missed a Benedictine basketball game. She always wore a beautiful red wool suit, which the kids called our good-luck suit. But when we went up to Atlanta for the state championships, I didn't expect to see her, because Atlanta's two hundred twenty-five miles away. She missed a couple of games, but when we got into the finals, I phoned and asked if she planned to come up. "I'll be there," she said.

The tournament was in Alexander Bell Memorial Coliseum at Georgia Tech, and our game, which started at nine, was the last one of the night. When we went out to warm up, we all looked for that red wool suit. The place was packed—it held seven thousand people—but my mama wasn't one of them. We looked and looked, but by game time there still wasn't a sign of her. We knelt for our prayer just before the tapoff—we always said the Lord's Prayer and a few Hail Marys—and just as we were about to start, I heard someone yelling, "Kenny, I'm here." I looked over, and there was my mama, dressed in her red wool suit, running down the steps of one of the aisles.

The kids gave a yell, and off we went on one of the best games we ever played. We won easily—I had 25 or 26 points—and the next day the Atlanta papers had a story about the mysterious lady in red who inspired the Benedictine Cadets to victory.

4 | Poolroom Adventures

I've been playing pool since I was eleven or twelve years old, and nobody can convince me that poolrooms are tough places for kids to hang out in. When I was a bratty little shoeshine boy in Savannah after my parents separated, the nicest guys I met were in a poolroom. One day I dragged my little shine box into one called the Sports Center. The owner was a guy named Sonny Linton, and instead of throwing me out he gave me a quarter to shine his shoes. He was always wonderful to me, and so were his customers. I could go into the Sports Center and make a whole day's pay with my shine box. And, in the natural course of events, I started learning how to handle a cue.

I could run the rack in nine-ball within a month after I learned the game. A natural aptitude for pool, a flock of willing tutors, and a real love for the game they taught me made me an expert at an age when most kids were playing with marbles. I'm not sure exactly how old I was when I started really spending a lot of time at the pool table, but I do know that I played hooky in favor of nine-ball regularly when I was in the seventh grade at Chatham Junior High. The school was only two blocks from the Sports Center. Sometimes I spent sixteen hours there—from eight in the morning until midnight.

Pool wasn't all I learned at the Sports Center. Besides pool-table etiquette—the game has one, believe it or not—I learned all about hustling: how to hustle, when, and under what conditions. Hustling is dirty pool. You look for a sucker, lose small amounts to him until he's convinced he can beat you, then get him up to higher stakes and murder him. You don't hustle friends or people you like. You don't hustle when you're among people who treat you respectably and don't expect you to hustle. In fact, you don't hustle under any conditions if you can help it—only if the other guy bugs you or tries to hustle you.

I have hustled guys when I felt it was warranted. And I have been accused of hustling when I really wasn't. Pool is like any other game—sometimes you're hot right from the start and sometimes it takes you a couple of games to warm up. There are times when the best of pool players is cold, but the longer he plays the hotter he gets. If he's really better than you are, he'll beat you eventually. That doesn't make him a hustler—only a slow starter.

Unless you can judge a stranger's real ability right from the beginning, it's dangerous to suggest higher stakes just because you beat him a few times. But a good pool player knows what he's up against right off. I can tell by watching a guy for only a couple of minutes, but I can't say exactly how. Maybe it's little mannerisms as he handles his cue, or the angles he uses, or even just the way he looks at the layout of balls on the table. Good pool players have no trouble measuring each other, even when they're strangers.

From the time I first began playing nine-ball, I was always looking for guys who were better than I was. That, of course, is the only way to learn any game. You can't learn anything from guys you can beat—I don't care if it's nine-ball, golf, tennis, bowling, whatever. I still look for better players, still will spend hours in a poolroom—knowing it's going to cost me money—but learning, always learning. And no matter how good you are, you'll never know all there is to know. You can always find somebody better, and when you do you'll come away from the game with something you didn't have when you went into it. What you lose is your tuition for the lesson you learned.

You almost always play for cash. Only with guys you play with regularly and know can be trusted do you use markers. Or if you're playing somebody you have every reason to believe is good for the money—a guy someone you trust vouches for, or maybe a rich local character who wants to be able to tell people he played you. I try hard to avoid situations like that unless the guy is really good.

When I first started playing for money I never had much cash, but that didn't bother me. I often went into the Sports Center with a quarter or fifty cents in my pocket and played the first game for a dollar. If I lost, we used markers. If I won, I'd collect right away. If I ended up losing more than I had, I'd pay off when I had the money. That didn't happen very often. I won most of the time.

As a kid, of course, I played for small potatoes. But after I was in pro ball, I won and lost in pretty big figures. I've won as much as twenty-two hundred dollars. The most I can remember losing was about nine hundred.

I remember one time when the Benedictine basketball team went up to Augusta for a two-day tournament. I was almost flat broke. We played afternoons, so the first night was free. Danny Shimkus, one of the kids on the team, had always heard me talk about what a good pool player I was—hiding my light under a bushel was never one of my long suits.

"How much dough have you got, Kenny?" he said.

"Couple of dollars," I said.

"You're such a great pool player," he said, "you ought to be able to run that up."

"Funny," I said. "I was thinking that very thing."

51

"Take me along," Danny said. "I've never seen you play."

So we went into this poolroom, and I found a guy about thirty looking for a game. This is practically a guarantee: there are always guys looking for games in poolrooms.

"How about a little nine-ball?" he said.

"I don't mind," I said.

"Five bucks a game?"

"Let's make it ten," I said.

"O.K.," the guy said.

Danny went white, but I just winked at him.

I won the break, ran the first three games without missing a shot, and the guy quit after paying off the thirty bucks. When we got outside Danny said, "Gawdalmighty, you're as good as you say you are. But tell me something. What would you have done if you lost the first game?"

"How much money have you?" I said.

"About ten bucks."

"I'd have paid him with that and given it back to you after I won it back," I said.

I would do better at nine-ball if I got the killer instinct more often—the instinct that makes you want to beat a guy's ass until you've got every cent he owns. Instead, I usually try to give a guy a chance to get his money back, like that time just before I had to go to the Blue-Gold football game when I played for the twenty-five bucks the guy owed me. I beat him and he paid me fifty, but we would have been even if he had beaten me. I don't know how many times I let guys off the hook that way.

Only once in a great while—when I'm mad at a guy or he has tried to ream me or made dirty cracks or called me a hustler or something—I get that killer instinct. One night in Savannah a guy I knew didn't like me started bugging me with smart cracks about how I wasn't half the pool player I thought I was. It was true. I was still spotty—nowhere near as consistent as a good pool player should be—and I knew he could beat me. I finally thought, *The hell with it,* and challenged him to nine-ball at ten bucks a game.

"Show me your dough, kid," he said.

I pulled four sawbucks out of my wallet—forty bucks—enough for four games.

"You wouldn't want to play for all of it at once, would you?" the guy said.

"The hell I wouldn't."

So we played one game for forty bucks and I won. Then we played for fifty a game and I kept right on winning. I ran my bankroll up to five hundred, and he wanted to play one game for that.

"Let me see your money," I said.

He didn't have any.

"We'll use markers," he said.

"Cash or nothing," I said, and walked away with his five hundred dollars. That was one of the few nights I can remember that I had the killer instinct.

Any time you play a guy for blood you have to be ready for a fight. I guess I've been in as many fights over pool as anything else. Sometimes they're my fault, sometimes the other guy's. Under any conditions, I don't get into fights with friends—people I play with regularly and with whom I enjoy mutual trust. Anyhow, I always figure the pool game is usually the excuse, not the reason, for a fight. When you don't like a guy or he doesn't like you, or you know you'd like to beat him up some time and that he feels the same way about you, sooner or later a fight is inevitable. But you just can't walk up to somebody, say, "I don't like you," and throw a punch. It takes more than that to start something. Any gambling game can do it, and nine-ball is a gambling game.

One night, after I had been playing about nine hours at a place in Savannah called Bo-Peep's, an older guy who I knew hated my guts came in and challenged me to nine-ball at five bucks a game. He was a better player, and I was sure he had a lot more dough than I did because I was down to about thirty bucks. But I had had a hot streak, so I figured maybe I could take him.

After about an hour, during which I had held my own, I realized I was pooped—after all, I hadn't done anything else but bend over pool tables for ten straight hours—and he started winning. I kept handing him five-dollar bills, but decided not to tell him when I was down to my last one. He took that, I kept right on going, and he beat me again. When I didn't pay him, he said, "Well?"

"I'm broke," I said. "I'll pay you tomorrow."

"The hell," he said. "I want my money."

"I'll get it later," I said. "Come on, let's keep going."

He was mad, but I finally not only talked him into playing some more, but got him to double up so I'd have a better chance of getting even. Instead, I kept right on losing, and pretty soon I was down about eighty bucks.

"All right," he said, "that does it. Go get some money if you want to play me any more."

"Come on over to the Sports Center," I said. "There are plenty of guys there who'll give me the dough." The Sports Center was closed and I knew it, so I was ready for trouble when we got there.

"Listen, kid," he said, "I want my money."

"Well, what the hell do you expect me to do?" I said. "I haven't got any. How am I going to pay you?"

"If you don't pay me, I'll take it right out of your ass," he said.

"That's all right with me," I said. "Start swinging."

And we went at it right on the street, clobbering the hell out of each other for about ten minutes before I could get him to quit.

"We're even," I said.

"O.K.," he said. "We're even."

You'd be surprised how many pool debts are settled that way.

There was one guy in Savannah—can't think of his name—whom I almost always played exactly even. We once went a hundred and thirty games, with each of us winning sixty-five. Since the loser pays for the use of the table—at the Sports Center it was a dime for nine-ball—we had to play one game to see who would pick up the tab. He beat me, so it cost me the $13.10 that went to the house.

One night in Pensacola—my first spring training in Florida—I went into a poolroom with some of the other kids on the ball club. A guy about twenty-five watched me play a minute and said, "How good are you?"

"Not bad," I said. "Not good. Just fair."

That was true enough at the moment. I didn't feel good—needed to get warmed up—and I wasn't doing too well.

"You want to play a little nine-ball?"

I was flat—I don't think I had two bucks in my pocket—but I said sure. We started playing for five bucks a game, and I was lousy. Fortunately, the other guy couldn't play at all, and I beat him out of a hundred without getting much better. After he paid me, another guy who had been watching us challenged me, and with a hundred-buck cushion I accepted.

I lost a couple of times, then began to loosen up, and pretty soon I was running one rack after another. I took the guy for maybe two hundred before he quit. As I put the last sawbuck in my wallet, the first guy came over and said, "I want my money back."

"What the hell are you talking about?" I said.

"This guy you just beat is one of the best players in Pensacola, and you told me you were only fair. You hustled me out of my hundred."

"What do you mean?" I said. "I was cold against you, and I got hot playing him."

"You hustled me, you bastard," the guy said. Then he picked up a ball and threw it at me. When I ducked it, he heaved a cue stick at me, yelling bloody murder and calling me all kinds of names. I ducked the stick, too, and by then the guy was close enough for me to drill him. I belted him in the mouth, and he went down still yelling. By then the joint was in an uproar and the poolroom owner, who knew I was a ballplayer, came over and said, "You'd better get the hell out of here. Somebody just called the police."

I never played pool in Pensacola again, but my conscience was clear. Whatever the guy thought, I hadn't hustled him—or at least not purposely.

After I got into pro baseball, one thing I really wanted to do was play in the annual ballplayers' golf tournament in Miami just before spring training starts. The big stars and the best golfers are invited down and get expenses while they're there, but in 1964 I was a twenty-two-year-old Kansas City rookie whom nobody had ever heard of and who was too broke to go anywhere until spring training officially began. For Betty Ann and me to go to Miami on our own would cost at least three hundred dollars, and we didn't have anywhere near that much to spare.

"Man, I sure wish we could go to Miami," I told her. "I could win that tournament."

"I wouldn't mind going to Miami myself," she said. "But what will we use for money?"

Well, we didn't have it, so that was that. The day before the Miami tournament opened, I had to go down to a photo studio on State Street to pick up some pictures. The place was right next door to the Sports Center, so naturally I dropped in, just to see if there might be a game around. I had about fifty bucks, which I couldn't afford to lose, but I always went into pool games expecting to win.

A really good friend of mine named Corky O'Neill—a red-headed, heavy-set fireman with whom I used to play ball in school —was looking for a game. The two of us must have played a million nine-ball games without more than twenty-five or thirty bucks ever changing hands, we were that evenly matched.

Everybody liked Corky. He was a nice guy and strictly on the level. Although he didn't have a very good job, he knew how to make a buck on the side, drove a nice car, and always carried plenty of cash. And he was one of those guys who, if he lost more than he had in his pocket, it was still money in the bank because he always paid off. When Corky saw me and suggested a nine-ball game, I naturally accepted. I didn't have anything else to do except maybe play golf.

We played for five dollars a game, and I started winning right off. Hot as I was, Corky was that cold, and pretty soon it was obvious that the only way he could get his dough back was by playing catchup. First he suggested we up the ante to ten bucks a game, then to twenty, and still I won. Actually, he was playing miserably, and when I had him up to six hundred, he said, "Kenny, this just isn't my day. I've got to quit."

"O.K.," I said, "give me what you can and owe me the rest."

"I'm not going to owe you anything," he said, and handed me six C-notes.

I drove home as fast as I could, walked into the house, and told Betty Ann, "Get packed, baby. We're going to Miami." I'll tell you about the tournament a little later.

I don't have that kind of luck very often, but I've had some real hot streaks. I once played nine-ball for ten bucks a game and walked out with sixty dollars without the other guy lifting his cue. I won the break and ran six racks in a row, so he never got a shot.

Every year people ask me why I'm not in the annual LaCosta golf tournament, run by American Airlines each January in San Diego. The reason is a nine-ball game I played with the wrong guy. If I had known what I was up against, I never would have accepted his challenge.

In the LaCosta, a pro baseball and a pro football player, usually from the same city, pair up, with the winners collecting good cash prizes and everyone having a great time. I was with the Washington Senators when I went out there for the 1967 tournament. I got friendly with a lot of pro football players, many of whom are pretty good pool players.

I played for small stakes, so nobody would get hurt. I had played a lot more than Johnny Unitas, Merlin Olsen, Lance Alsworth, and guys like that, and I didn't want to take their money. I was beating them all, and after a while I noticed this guy always watching us.

One day, without looking at any of us directly, he said, "I want to play some pool. I play very well and I can beat anyone here. Anybody care to take me on?"

"Here's a man who'll play you," Unitas said. "He's as good as anyone I've ever seen."

The guy said, "O.K."

"O.K.," I said. "But I want you to understand that I grew up on this game and I'm pretty sure I can beat you."

"We'll see about that," the guy said. "How about nine-ball, twenty dollars a game?"

That was fine with me. He won a few games while I was warming up, and when he ran me up to a hundred dollars, I knew I could beat him and said, "Do you want to play for more?"

"Fifty a game all right with you?" he said.

So we played for fifty dollars a game. I started killing him— boom, boom, boom, one game after another—and he quit, owing me six hundred fifty dollars. He left without paying me, after telling me he'd see me the next day out at LaCosta, where he was a member. I wasn't crazy about not collecting on the spot, but I figured any member of LaCosta would be good for a six-hundred-fifty-dollar gambling debt.

When I saw him at the club the next day he didn't say anything, and he didn't say anything the day after, or on the last day of the tournament. By this time I had found out he was a big-shot businessman and one of the most prominent members of the club, and I was pretty mad about his not paying me.

On the last day, one of the ballplayers who knew him took me over to his office just before I was to catch a plane back to Washington. When I walked in, I said, "How about that money you owe me?"

"Why don't I give you two-fifty now," he said, "and I'll send the rest later?"

"Look," I said, "I've been told you're a pretty substantial guy with a good reputation around town. You lost six hundred and fifty to me. Why don't you just go ahead and give me the whole thing?"

"Frankly," he said, "because my wife will get sore if she sees one big check made out to you. She'll know I lost it gambling. I'll give you two-fifty now, and mail you the other four hundred in a couple of days."

It was an old story that I had heard a dozen times—only not from guys in his obviously lush financial condition—and I figured I'd better take what I could get and run. So I said, "O.K., give me a check for whatever you want and send the rest to me, care of the Washington Senators."

He gave me two hundred fifty dollars and I was so mad I walked out without even shaking hands. And all the way to the airport I griped about what kind of members they had at that swanky LaCosta club.

I never heard from the guy again, and the next year American Airlines didn't invite me back. No explanation, no nothing—just

59

no invitation. I finally found out what happened from Unitas. After that pool game, the guy went to the tournament committee and said, "If you ever invite Harrelson here again I'm resigning my membership in the club. This man's a pool hustler. I don't want him back here."

Every ballplayer who saw me play that guy—and there were plenty of them, including Unitas—knew I hadn't hustled him. He was the one who insisted on playing. I had warned him before we started that I could beat him. When I suggested we up the stakes, he had made it fifty dollars, knowing I'd probably beat him. And after he quit, he welshed on four hundred of the six-fifty I beat him for.

I wanted badly to go back to LaCosta because it was a real fun tournament. I tried to reach Bob Bushnell, the tournament director, five straight days to find out why I hadn't been asked. Later, when Unitas told me the story, I realized Bushnell had been ducking me, and neither he nor anyone else at American Airlines had ever bothered to hear my side.

But during the 1968 baseball season, they had the guts to ask me to cooperate on a feature story with my picture on the front cover of their house organ. I told them where they could shove that. If they listen to a guy who welshes on a legitimate gambling debt and blackball the man he welshed on, I want no part of them or their tournament. I'll never play in it again without apologies from the airline and the automobile dealer who branded me a hustler—to say nothing of the money he still owes me. I'm sorry I didn't follow my lawyer's advice and sue him for defamation of character. I had so many witnesses who knew the real story that it would have cost him a hell of a lot more than the four hundred dollars he still owes me.

5 | Bitten by the Golf Bug

When I fell in love with golf I worked harder at it than any other game I've ever played except baseball. I wanted to become not just a good golfer but an outstanding one. The fact that I was off to such a late start made it necessary for me to work that much harder. I mapped out a careful campaign that I hoped would put me in the same class with the best golfers in Savannah and maybe well beyond Savannah.

My idol was Hobart Manley, one of the finest amateurs in the country, who lived in Savannah. He had won important tournaments all over the East, and once beat Billy Joe Patton in the North-South Open. He's not only a great golfer, but a great guy. Everybody in Savannah is in love with him. A real sweetheart, nice to everyone in spite of his social and financial standing, both of which are very high, Hobart was everything I ever wanted to be. I admire him as much today as when I was a kid, and I never go to Savannah that I don't spend some time, on or off the golf course, with him.

Hobart was a key figure in my campaign to become a good golfer. Since he was the best one in Savannah, I wanted to watch him as much as possible. The easiest way to do it would have been to caddie for him, but he had a regular caddie. I did the next best thing—caddied as often as possible for Bob White, with whom Hobart often played.

Besides being my idol, Hobart became my model. I watched every move he made, practiced swinging like him in front of a mirror every night. Hobart could hit a ball a mile. I wanted to outhit him. He could consistently score in the low 70s. I wanted to outscore him. He had a great short game. I wanted to develop a better one. He was a fine putter, but I wasn't worried about outputting him. Years of miniature golf had made a pretty good putter out of me, and I think I could outputt him from the start.

Watching and learning to imitate Hobart Manley was only part of my campaign. I never missed a golf show on television, so I could watch the pros. If someone had a move that I thought would help my game, I imitated it. You can always get tips on golf from experts, and tips come a dime a dozen when the pros are on television.

And of course I played—every day and for as long as I could. When I play tournament golf today, I hate to go more than eighteen holes because I think that's as much concentrated golf as anyone can take in one day. But when there's nothing at stake I'll play until I drop. I've often played thirty-six holes of fun golf in a day. A couple of years ago I went forty-five with Paul Richards, an old golfing pal of mine who is now general manager of the Atlanta Braves. And there were days when, as a sixteen-year-old in Savannah, I played forty-five holes.

While I was learning the game I always played alone. I didn't want anyone to see me flubbing shots, or skipping the ball along the ground, or missing it altogether. I played four or five balls on every hole, carefully keeping scores and notations on what I did right and wrong. I had a natural swing and could hit like hell off the tees, but I was wild, often hooking or slicing or shanking my tee shots. I did better on calm days than windy ones because I hit a high shot which would be held back by a strong wind. My irons weren't good. Irons are the trickiest shots in golf because they must be carefully controlled. You can't simply stand there and smash the ball the way you can with woods. You have to hit it just right—not too strong and not too weak. Hitting an iron properly requires as much concentration as putting.

Like all kids, I always wanted to kill the ball. To me, there was no thrill greater than watching a tee shot go out of sight and know it was way the hell and gone down the fairway. That's what I liked about Hobart Manley's tee shots—he could absolutely murder the ball. While caddying in any foursome he was in, I measured his tee shots, marking where they landed. Hobart Manley was the longest hitter in Savannah. When I was ready, I wanted to get into a driving contest with him, because if I outdrove him I'd be the longest hitter in Savannah.

Golf is an expensive game, but it didn't cost me much once I had my clubs. I hitchhiked out to the Mary Calder golf course, where Leo Beckman, the pro, let me play for nothing. Club pros are like that—when they see a kid with real desire and dedication to the game they help him out. I played hundreds of rounds at Mary Calder without its costing me a dime. I used balls I found on the course, at Mary Calder or wherever else I might be caddying. There are always stray golf balls around. Guys lose them, drop another, and forget about them. In one round. I could find enough balls to keep me going for the next three.

Three months after I played my first round with Floyd Doss and the kids from the Junior Legion team, I was down in the 90s regularly, and not until then did I go out with anyone else. By that time I knew I wouldn't flub shots very badly, and I could see my own improvement all the time. But I couldn't consider myself a really good golfer until I broke 80, and that took another two months. Six months to the day after my first round I shot a par 72 at Mary Calder. Only then did I figure I was ready for Hobart Manley.

HAWK

Although I often caddied in his foursomes, I still hardly knew him. He was always nice and friendly, called me by name and all that, but otherwise he didn't pay any more attention to me than most golfers pay to caddies. I always commented on the length of his drives and made remarks about how I wished I could hit the ball that far, but I don't think he realized how hard I worked to model myself after him.

And I'm sure he didn't know how badly I wanted to beat him off the tee. Here I was, a poor kid just turned seventeen, and there he was, rich, handsome, capable, one of the most popular guys in Savannah, and the fresh kid was just aching to match him, tee shot for tee shot. Even after I felt I was ready, it took ingenuity just to get him into a driving contest. I couldn't go up to him and say, "Hobart, how about a contest?" He'd laugh at me.

One day, after playing a round with a couple of kids from school at the Savannah Golf Club, I noticed Hobart all alone on the practice tee. Except for a caddie to shag balls for him, there wasn't a soul within hailing distance. I wandered over with my bag on my shoulder and said, "Hobart, would you help me out a little, give me some tips on driving?"

"Sure," he said. "I'll hit a few and you hit a few, and if I can help you, fine."

His practice bag was lying on the ground with a whole flock of brand new Titlists rolling out of it. I thought of all my beat-up balls that I'd picked up on courses around town, and it just didn't seem right that I should try to hit those while Hobart was hitting his nice new ones. So when he had hit a couple of drives and stepped back to make room for me, I decided to use his Titlists instead of my crumby balls.

To the left of the practice tee was a cemetery, protected by a high fence. A tee shot in there was not only out of bounds but gone. You had to climb the fence to get in and climb it again to get out. The caddies—myself included—had a thing about that cemetery. Nobody wanted to go in there after a golf ball.

As I reached for one of those beautiful new Titlists, I suddenly felt very nervous. What the hell was I doing trying to outdrive the best amateur golfer in Savannah? What right did I have to think I could hit a ball farther than he could? And even if I did outdrive him, what would it prove?

My hand shook a little as I teed the ball up. I stood in front of it, feet wide apart, left elbow and right knee stiff, and took a couple of practice swings. Then I moved closer, brought the club back, took a mighty swipe . . . and belted the ball ten miles into the cemetery.

Automatically I reached for another Titlist—and socked that into the cemetery. After I hit a few more in there, I knew Hobart was ready to say, "Get your fresh ass out of here. While you're practicing, you're losing all my new golf balls."

I didn't give him a chance to say anything. I simply stepped aside and said, "Why don't you hit a few and let me watch you?"

While he was slamming three or four beautiful shots right down the middle, I lost that nervous feeling and got my confidence back. Finally, I said, "Mind if I try again, Hobart?"

"Go ahead," he said.

That time my drive went high up, far and straight as could be. I hit a couple more then, for maybe fifteen minutes, the two of us took turns, with everything going well down the fairway.

As a contest, it was probably a standoff. We never did actually measure our drives because the caddie was shagging everything for us. But we were both well aware that it *was* a contest, and that my asking him to help me had been just a blind. If I had any doubts about his not realizing I meant it to be a contest, they were dispelled when he said, "Kenny, how about playing a round with me next week? I think you're ready. And it will be interesting to see which one of us can hit the ball farther."

That was the real beginning of any ambitions I might ever have had to play serious golf. Hobart Manley's recognition of me—young as I was—as a worthy opponent for him made me in Savannah golfing circles. If Hobart would play me, anybody would, and I became part of the Savannah golf scene.

The best golfers in town played weekend tournaments called the Blitz. Fifty or sixty guys would come out every Saturday and Sunday, playing foursomes. The best man was the captain, followed by number-two, number-three, and number-four players. When I first started I was number four, and the one thing I wanted more than anything else was to be the captain. It took maybe six months for me to make it. By then, I was consistently in the low 70s, and sometimes in the 60s, and a hopeless golf buff.

We had some pretty big tournaments in Savannah, occasionally attracting the top pros, but the most popular player was always Hobart. No matter how well-known a golfer was, he drew the biggest galleries. Even when the pro circuit was around Savannah, more people followed Hobart than anyone else. He once nearly outdrew Arnie Palmer's army when Palmer played in Savannah.

He still outdraws everybody who comes to town. They had a big shindig for me in February 1969, after my great year with the Red Sox. I'd had all the publicity in the world. Between my clothes and my great season in 1968, I was all over the sports pages and magazines, and even hit some front covers.

The big event of my homecoming was a golf tournament. Here was the home-town boy who had really made it big—Hawk Harrelson, famous wherever people talk about sports, the great ballplayer, baseball's champion golfer, the mod dresser, the mop-haired character—and when he went out to play a round of golf on one of those Savannah courses where he learned the game, he figured to outdraw everybody.

He did—except Hobart Manley. Even on that biggest day of my life in my own home town, Hobart had a bigger following.

And I didn't begrudge him a thing. Because if I hadn't been playing, I would have been in his gallery myself.

I like having a gallery, because it makes me play better golf. I can't stand looking lousy in front of anybody. The more people watching, the better I feel. It's like baseball. When you have a poor crowd there's less incentive and you don't do so well. Not that you don't try just as hard or hustle just as much, but a big crowd gives you an added lift.

After joining the Red Sox, I didn't play nearly as much golf as I used to. Right up through 1966, I was out on the course every chance I had. When we played a night game or had an off day, I spent hours playing golf. After day games, I dressed as fast as I could to get out on the course for nine or eighteen holes before dark.

A guy doing that all the time can't do justice to baseball. The trouble was, I always played for losers—the Kansas City Athletics and the Washington Senators. Neither team was going anywhere, and it didn't look as if I was either. This made golf that much more important to me. I might not have knocked anybody dead on the ballfield—although, believe me, I had some great days with Kansas City and Washington—but I was a consistent winner in golf.

When I was concentrating on golf, I could beat anyone on a given day, including guys who have made it big on the pro circuit. A couple of years before he won the National Open I beat Lee Trevino. I don't know how many times I've broken 70 on championship courses. I once had a one-foot putt for a 64, and I've had at least half a dozen 65s. This was when I really worked at golf, both in and out of the baseball season. I play only in the off-season now, and that comparatively little, since there's no golf around Boston in the winter. Naturally, my game has suffered. I never broke 70 after joining the Red Sox.

But I can come back quickly. I played only a couple of rounds in Savannah before barely losing the 1969 baseball players' golf championship in Miami. If I concentrated on golf, I could make a good living on the pro circuit. There was a time when I seriously considered joining it, especially when I played for Washington, where I was very unhappy. In fact, until 1967 I wavered between baseball and golf for years.

Give me a couple of weeks' practice and there are guys who'll still bet a fortune on me in a golf match. I once played a nine-hole match at the Canyon Country Club in Palm Springs, California, against another ballplayer for five thousand dollars. I didn't have that kind of money, but a guy backed me, and if we won *I'd* have collected half the winnings. Par for nine holes was 36. I shot a 34, but the other guy was hotter. He beat me by a stroke.

With others sharing the risk, I've bet as much as six thousand dollars on a golf match. I wouldn't do that unless I was playing really well—and when I'm that good I don't lose very much or very often. When you bet all that money, it's not just on the match. There are so many ways to bet on golf that you never lose everything if you're on your game. On Nassau, for example, where you're making separate bets on the front nine, the back nine, and the whole eighteen, you're almost sure to win one of them.

One year, when I didn't go over 71 more than half a dozen times in a month, the only way I could lose was when somebody played way over his head. One day I shot a 68 on a course where the record was 67—and got beaten when my opponent had a record-breaking 66. It was the first time all year he had been under 70. Believe me, that was an expensive round.

I got it all back at Blue Hills in Kansas City one day when I had seven birdies and an eagle for a 67 that broke the course record by two strokes. We were playing two hundred dollar Nassau and four hundred dollars for the eighteen, with gimmicks like automatic presses that zoomed the stakes up into the thousands. I won everything that time.

I've had some wonderful times and met some wonderful people through golf. One of my favorite tournaments was at Palm Springs, where a lot of show-business people play. Chuck Connor's house is on the twelfth or thirteenth fairway. Every time we went by we'd run in for a beer. He had a refrigerator stocked with it just for golfers.

David Janssen, who played "The Fugitive," is a strong guy. Once I putted out on the tenth hole and, while I was waiting for Peanuts Lowrey to putt, I watched Janssen swinging about three hundred yards back on the fairway. The ball rolled right up by the hole before Lowrey putted.

Of course, I can talk big about winning this tournament or that one, and about holding my own with the pros if I concentrated on golf, but the one tournament where I've ever been consistently successful is the annual baseball championship in Miami. I won it three years out of four, and in 1969 blew a two-stroke lead on the thirty-sixth hole, then lost to Sammy Ellis of the White Sox in a sudden-death playoff.

By then, I was well established, but no golf people had ever heard of me when I made my first baseball tournament in 1964. I was known only among ballplayers because I had broken the Eastern League record in home runs and runs-batted-in a couple of years before.

After winning that six hundred dollars from Corky O'Neill in the pool game at the Sports Center and telling Betty Ann to get packed, I phoned the Lejeune Country Club in Miami to let them know I was coming.

"This is Ken Harrelson of the Athletics," I said.

"Who?" the guy asked.

"Harrelson. Ken Harrelson. I'm with Kansas City. I want to play in the tournament."

"It starts in the morning," the guy said. "Can you make it?"

"I live in Savannah," I said.

"All right. We'll enter you. Check in at the Green Mansions Motel."

Betty Ann and I packed as fast as we could—threw things into the trunk of the car, and took off at about six o'clock. Just before we got out of Savannah I said, "Did we pack everything?"

"Yes," she said, "don't worry about anything. It's all packed. All your clothes and everything."

We talked about one thing and another as we drove south. After we had gone about a hundred fifty miles—we were just past Jacksonville—I had a horrible thought.

"Betty Ann," I said, "did you pack my golf clubs?"

"I thought *you* packed them."

"I didn't pack them," I said. "Damn, I must have left them on the back porch."

We had gone too far and it was too late to turn back, so I knew I'd have to borrow clubs. I hoped there'd be time because I wouldn't know what time I would tee off until I got there. By going like hell—it's normally about eleven hours from Savannah to Miami—I pulled into the motel at three in the morning, leaving a call for seven.

It was lucky I made it early. When I got over to Lejeune, I found I was scheduled to tee off at eight. I went over to the assistant pro, a guy about sixty or so, and said, "Look, I left my clubs at home. Can I borrow a set here?"

"You can take mine, if you like," he said.

I thanked him, and took his clubs right out to the first tee because there wasn't time even to hit a few drives off the practice tee. I played with Jim Hearn, Kenny Johnson, and a fourth guy whose name slips my mind. I had never met any of them, although I knew Hearn and Johnson by reputation. All we had time to do before teeing off was shake hands and get going.

70

I wasn't happy with my borrowed clubs. The shafts were whippy and I use a stiff shaft, because the stronger you are, the stiffer the shaft should be. I thought about looking for another set after the round, but I shot a 75, so I decided to stay with them. The only guy to outscore me was Albie Pearson, then the smallest man in the majors, and one of the game's best golfers. He was 74 or 73.

The next day I had another 75, and was still second to Pearson, two strokes off his pace. Ralph Terry of the Yankees was a stroke behind me, and Alvin Dark, who then managed the Giants, was one behind him and four behind Pearson.

Now everybody knew Hawk Harrelson. Newspapermen from all over the country interviewed me, and I was on nation-wide radio and people were talking about me. From a baseball standpoint, I was nothing—a rookie with a ball club going nowhere. But as a golfer, I was suddenly very big indeed—a kid playing with borrowed clubs right up among the leaders.

The tournament was rained out the third day, and it had to end the fourth, a Sunday. George Jacobus, the tournament director, called Pearson, Terry, Dark, and me, the only ones with a chance to win, and said, "Do you guys want to play eighteen holes or thirty-six?"

Alvin, who knew he couldn't make up four strokes on Pearson in eighteen holes, said, "I'd like to play thirty-six."

Both Pearson and Terry said they didn't care. As the youngest and least known, I was the last one asked.

"I want to play eighteen," I said. "I don't like to play thirty-six holes of pressure golf in one day."

Alvin, whom I had never met before, gave me a dirty look, as Jacobus said, "I've got one guy wants to play thirty-six, one wants to play eighteen, and two who don't give a damn. What are we going to do?"

"Well, I don't want to play thirty-six," I said.

Pearson, who had everything to gain by playing only eighteen holes, said, "O.K. Let's play eighteen." When Terry agreed, Jacobus said, "Eighteen it is then."

That was the first time I met Alvin Dark. We later became the closest of friends, and today, we're like father and son. But that day I was just a fresh rookie who had got his way over three veterans, and I guess he hated my guts.

We played threesomes, and I teed off with Pearson and Terry. It was the first time I had ever played before a gallery—we must have had three thousand people following us, mostly to watch Albie. The weather was warm, but very windy, and Albie played as well as I've ever seen anyone play on a day like that. He shot line drives off the tee, and they cut through the wind for maximum distance. He ended up with a 70, which was phenomenal in that weather. I don't think any pro would have done any better.

I couldn't keep the ball down at all, especially with those whippy clubs. Every wood shot I hit went sky high, but nowhere near as far as usual, and I finished with a 78. That was good enough for second place, because both Terry and Dark were in the 80s.

Although Pearson won the tournament, I think I got more prizes because Jacobus liked me. He had taken such a shine to me that he showered me with prizes—a video tape recorder, a camera, a television monitor, a diamond stickpin, a set of matched luggage, a diamond charm for Betty Ann, and a few other things I can't remember. I never collected that much loot for winning.

The next year, 1965, the tournament committee gave me the full treatment. They phoned several days in advance to invite me down in time for a couple of practice rounds at the Miami Springs Country Club, where the tournament had been shifted from Lejeune. They paid all expenses for Betty Ann and me, and promised that this time I'd be assigned a more reasonable hour to tee off than eight in the morning.

Naturally, I was delighted. As usual, I was broke and would have hesitated to go down on my own account without another successful trip to the Sports Center. Although I'd been in and out of Kansas City the year before, I still hadn't made it permanently to the majors and was collecting a minimum salary out of baseball. We got through the winter on golf and nine-ball.

Half a dozen newspapermen, mostly from Miami, followed me on my practice round two days before the tournament began. When we finished and were sitting around in the clubhouse, one of the writers said, "You were a surprise runner-up last year, Hawk. How do you think you'll do this time?"

"I'll win it," I said. "Nobody can beat me."

And that was the headline on the Miami sports pages the next day: "NOBODY CAN BEAT ME," SAYS THE HAWK.

I was having lunch with Pearson, Terry, Dark, and a couple of other guys and one of them, after looking at the paper, said, "Hawk, did you really say that?"

"Why, yes," I said.

"Would you like to bet on it?"

"Sure."

Pearson, Terry, and I each put up one hundred dollars—Alvin never made more than small token bets—with the winner to collect it all. From then on, I took a pretty good ribbing, both from other ballplayers and the gallery, but that didn't bother me. I had been playing very well, and was sure I really would win. I played in the same foursome with Dark the first two days, and on the last two with Terry and Pearson.

Coming down to the last day, the same four of us were in the lead. I was two strokes up on Pearson, with Terry third and Dark fourth. When Albie, Ralph, and I teed off, there must have been seven thousand in the gallery that followed us. Ham that I am, I was right in my element. I loved every minute of it.

The pressure was all on me. I had said I'd win, had bet on

myself, was in front going into the final eighteen holes, and I looked about twice as big as Albie. So, although he was the defending champion, he was still the sentimental favorite, the appealing little underdog trying to beat the big bad giant.

I lost my two strokes on the first two holes because Albie parred the first while I bogied it and he birdied the second while I parred it. I got my two strokes back on the third, an unusually long par 3, which I parred while Albie was getting a double bogie. When I picked up three more strokes on the next five holes, giving me a five-stroke lead on the ninth tee and needing only a par for a 34, I figured I was home free. Terry and Dark had fallen far behind, leaving Pearson the only one for me to beat.

The ninth at Miami Springs is a par 4. Albie hit a great drive, leaving himself an easy iron shot to the green. My tee shot hit a tree and dropped half-buried behind a root. All I had was the top of the ball for a target, and the best I could do was move it maybe a foot and a half for a better lie. But I was right behind a tree and had to cut the ball, which landed to the right of the green.

So there I was, still off the green in three, while Albie sat eight feet from the pin in two. I got on in four, leaving myself a twelve-foot putt, but it took me three to sink the damn ball for a seven. Albie got his birdie three and now my five-stroke lead had shrunk to one.

The crowd was buzzing, and gave me a mock cheer when I finally putted out. I should have been madder than hell, but I was still so sure I'd win that I felt pretty good. As I reached down to take my ball out of the cup, I looked at Albie and winked at him. He grinned, but I knew he was surprised. That wink gave me a psychological advantage because he had expected me to blow my stack after butchering the hole so badly. Now he realized I was still completely relaxed and as confident as ever.

I got one stroke back in the next four holes, and was two up again as we went to the fourteenth tee. This was an easy par 5, because a good drive left you with a 3- or 4-iron shot to the green. Albie hit a beauty, right down the fairway. I don't know what happened to me—I topped the ball and it went into the rough, maybe two hundred yards from the tee. With about three hundred to go, I had to use a 3 wood to get any distance out of that guck. It was an easy one to mess up, but I just hit the hell out of the ball. It landed on the green ten feet short of the cup, one of the greatest shots I ever made in my life. Albie birdied the hole, but I sank my putt for an eagle and went three strokes up on him. He got one back on the seventeenth, and we went to the eighteenth, just where we had started, with me two strokes in front.

With victory in sight, I suddenly got the jitters. Here was this big crowd, rooting harder than ever for Li'l Albie, and here I was with a two-stroke lead, scared to death I'd blow it, the way I had blown the ninth. The eighteenth was a short par 4, easy if you hit the ball straight, but tough as hell if you hooked because there was trouble on the left. I had hooked several tee shots already. Albie had been accurate with his drives and was great from tee to green because he had a marvelous iron game—one of the best I've ever seen. His only weakness was putting, but this didn't hurt him as much as it might because he usually got his irons almost dead to the pin. My putting, usually very good, had been off, so I had every reason to be nervous.

Albie, who had won the seventeenth, hit first, a beauty right down the chute. I got up there, saying to myself, *Hawk, damn you, this is your last one. Make it good.* With my adrenalin running and my nerves all keyed up, I reared back and belted a fantastic drive—straight down the middle, eighty yards past Albie and an easy little wedge shot to the green.

Albie, his irons as good as ever, was on in two, maybe eight feet from the pin. I walked over to my ball, pulled out my wedge—

75

and froze. My short game had been lousy all day. There were all those people crowded behind me, most of them hoping I'd flub the shot, and I wasn't sure I wouldn't. I could be too short or too long, or need three to get on the green, or lick myself with one putt too many—there were so many ways I could lose this thing.

As I bent over the ball with the wedge in my hand, I said to myself, *All you've got to do is knock this little bitty shot up to the green and you'll win the tournament,* but I couldn't make myself swing the club. While the crowd watched and Albie waited, I must have stood over that ball for five full minutes.

I looked at the ball and I looked at the green. I saw Albie's ball up there and I kept swinging the wedge gently back and forth and, somehow or other, I just couldn't make myself make that shot. Even though I kept telling myself it was easy, I was afraid I'd shank it and maybe land in a trap or ruin myself with a bad lie.

Nobody knew what was going on in my mind. There wasn't a sound from the crowd. The people just stood there and waited, wondering when I was going to get around to hitting that ball. I didn't want to hit it. All I wanted to do was walk away.

Finally I thought, *The hell with it,* swung the wedge, and stiffed it. The ball stopped dead three feet from the pin, and I was home. Albie met me at the edge of the green, because the minute I hit the ball he knew it was all over. A perfect gentleman, he said, "I'll putt out and then you putt. The champion should be the last one to take his ball out of the cup."

He sank his eight-footer for a birdie—and I missed my three-footer. It didn't matter, of course. The ball rimmed the cup, and I dropped it in for a par 4, winning by one stroke instead of two—but winning.

I hadn't finished in a blaze of glory, but it was enough. I looked like hell, with the bill of my hat sticking up and my huge nose peeling from sunburn, and I was still shaking from that attack of nerves, but I felt wonderful. Everybody congratulated me—Albie again, Ralph, Alvin, and all the others. It was great being the champion, even though I knew it all the time.

When they called me the next year—1966—and said, "Hawk, you'll be down for the tournament, won't you?", I said, "Sure, I'll be there. What have you got for a first prize?"

"All kinds of stuff—luggage, a big trophy, a perpetual-motion bell-shaped clock, the works."

"Just put it all off in a corner for me," I said. "I'll pick it up when the tournament's over."

When I arrived in Miami I asked a committee member, "What's the tournament record?"

"Two ninety-five," he said.

"Forget it," I said, "I'll break it."

Naturally, that got into the papers—HAWK PREDICTS NEW RECORD—and there I was on the spot again.

The night before the tournament began, Art Bruns, who owned the Miami Springs Villas, where a lot of us stayed, threw a big party for us. There must have been fifty baseball people around— Albie, Ralph, Alvin, Paul Richards, Mickey Mantle, Jackie Brandt, Yogi Berra, Whitey Ford, the whole gang.

Some member of the club, whose name I forget, got up and said, "I'm taking the Hawk for anything anyone wants to bet."

Another guy, who had been playing with Terry and knew he was hot, said, "I'll bet two thousand on Terry."

"Make it three," my guy said, "and you've got a bet."

I saw all this money flying around, so I jumped up and said, "Hell, man, I'm giving odds. I'll give two to one on myself." Everybody in the joint broke up, and I didn't get any takers at first. But I ended up with three or four, giving two hundred dollars to one hundred. Of course, Pearson, Terry, and I set up another three-hundred-dollar winner-take-all kitty, and we also bet a hundred on each round. Then I began talking about breaking the tournament record, and the next thing I knew guys were giving me odds I wouldn't. That gave me a whole flock of new bets—so many I had to write them all down to keep track of them.

I was setting myself up for lifelong poverty if I lost the works. With a bankroll of about two hundred and fifty dollars, I must have had five thousand bucks riding on myself.

The guy who had bet three thousand on me came over later and said, "If you win, you get half of it."

The first day was beautiful: the sun was shining, the wind gentle, the course in great shape. I had been playing the best golf of my life all winter and figured I'd build up a big lead right at the start, and just keep adding to it as we went along.

So what did I do on that gorgeous opening day? Fiddled and faddled around on a few holes and shot a lousy 76. It still left me in second place, only a stroke behind Pearson, but it wasn't anywhere near a record-breaking pace.

The second day it was pouring, but they wouldn't call it off. Like stupid idiots, the whole crowd of us went out, getting more and more drenched as we went along. I was in a foursome with Billy Herman, who walked off the course at the ninth green, saying, "The hell with this. I'm not going to get pneumonia." I don't know how many other guys did that, but I didn't. I was hot—out in 35, even though my caddie had to keep running back and forth to the pro shop to get me dry gloves and towels. I must have used twenty gloves that day, but I shot a 72 to go way out in front, because I don't think anyone else in the whole field broke 80.

That guy who had bet three thousand dollars followed me around, rain and all. He was still with me the next day, when the weather was just as bad. The rain came slanting down in buckets, but the committee still wouldn't postpone. I got soaked, used up about twenty more gloves, and shot another 72. My guy went all the way with me again.

Now I was twelve strokes in front of the field, and I would have had to curl over and die to lose. The sun finally came out on the fourth day, and a good gallery followed me when I went off the first tee. After I drove, I looked around, but my guy wasn't in sight. He had stayed with me for three rounds, two on the worst days I ever played golf, but he wasn't with me this time, and never did join me.

I bogied the first hole, then shot a 70, winning everything except that hundred to Albie when he beat me on the first round. I had a 290 total to break the tournament record by five strokes and had a record-breaking seventeen-stroke lead on the field at the finish.

Once in the clubhouse, I was busy collecting from everyone— everyone but that guy who had promised me half if he won his three thousand on me. I looked all over the place but didn't see him until the next year. Then he came over and said, "You know what happened to me last year? That old bastard who bet on Terry never paid me. He died about a month later."

"Man, get off my ass," I said. "I don't want your money. Just forget it."

Now I had won two tournaments in a row, and I should have been as confident as ever when I went down in 1967. But I had noticed that Sammy Ellis was getting better and better. He had the strokes, the temperament, and the desire, and that's a pretty tough combination to beat.

After the 1966 tournament, I had said to him, "Don't you worry about a thing, big boy. You keep working on your game and you'll be a hell of a player. Next year you can win this tournament."

"How the hell can I beat you guys?" he said. "I had four eighties, and finished forty strokes behind you."

"Believe me," I said. "You can beat us all next year."

But, although I hadn't been playing well, I couldn't go down there and not predict I'd win. I was the defending champion for the second year in a row, and there didn't seem to be anyone with a chance to beat me but Terry. Pearson was out of baseball and

Dark, then managing the Athletics, told me frankly that he didn't think he could concentrate enough on golf to win the thing.

Nowhere near as cocky as usual, I made some fairly sizable bets on myself—anything over a couple of hundred was more than I could afford—but I figured I could at least break even. One guy had a big thing for Davie Johnson, a hell of a fine player, but without much tournament experience. Besides, he got too red-ass on the golf course—blew sky-high when things went wrong. When this guy wanted to make a big bet—a thousand bucks, I think it was—that I couldn't beat Johnson, I grabbed it. I wouldn't have been that confident in a casual round with Davie, but I was sure I could beat him in tournament golf.

That bet saved my life. I never was under 75 and finished fourth at 306. I got some satisfaction out of the fact that my boy, Sammy Ellis, was the winner, finishing four strokes ahead of Alvin Dark. Joel Horlen was third, one stroke ahead of me. But in spite of all my lousy bets on myself, I won money because I beat Davie Johnson. Believe me, it wasn't easy. He was only one stroke behind me and almost surely would have beaten me except for his tendency to blow up—an 80 on the first round and a 79 on the fourth killed him. I don't know what happened to Terry. He wasn't even in the first ten.

The 1968 tournament was the first I ever entered with my mind clear of money worries. By then I was with the Red Sox, and loaded. I didn't make a single bet I couldn't have paid off if I lost. I had a big bonus, a great salary, World Series money, off-season deals, the works.

I also had confidence, thanks to Jim Ferree, the pro at the Savannah Country Club, who had played with me for a week before the tournament. Although hitting the ball well, I wasn't scoring, but Jim told me not to worry.

"How can I beat Ellis and Johnson this year?" I said.

"You'll beat them, Hawk," he said. "I know you will. You're a ballplayer—I'm a golfer. I've played Miami Springs. It's four strokes easier than this course. The way you're hitting the ball, nobody is going to beat you."

On the strength of Ferree's opinion alone, I picked myself and bet on myself, but I really thought Ellis would win. For two rounds, he and I were exactly even—we both started with 76s and then had 79s. But he blew up to an 81 in the third round. I had a 75, and that was my lead going into the last round—six strokes. I breezed home in 77 for a winning total of 307, seven strokes up on Jack Sanford, who nosed Ellis out for second place. So that year, needing money like a hole in the head, I won everything.

I really blew the 1969 tournament, the first one in six years in which I didn't pick myself to win. I had played very little golf all winter—a few rounds with Alvin Dark in his home town of Lake Charles, Louisiana, and a few more in Savannah, just before going to Miami. And when I got there, I picked Sammy Ellis.

He beat me the hard way. I led him by three strokes going into the last round. He was in the foursome ahead of me, and when I reached the seventeenth tee, I was two strokes up on him. Just before I teed the ball up, word came back that Sammy had sunk a twenty-footer for a birdie and a 306 total. All I needed to beat him was a par four. But I bogied the damn hole and blew the tournament on the extra hole when Ellis sank a forty-five-foot putt for another birdie. I hate like hell to lose, but at least the guy who beat me was the one I picked.

6 | Everything but Baseball

As long as I can remember I've been nuts about cars. I've been driving since I was big enough to reach the brake with my foot, and I've handled everything from jalopies to Jaguars. Poor as we were—and there were times when things were pretty bad for us around Savannah—we always had some kind of car. I didn't get to use it much because my mama or my sister needed it, but they were pretty good about letting me borrow it from time to time.

One of my dearest ambitions was to buy a Cadillac for my mama. She's like me—she loves cars, the nicer the better. When I first signed a baseball contract with the Kansas City club I bought her a Pontiac and said, "This is nothing, Mama. Someday I'll give you a Cadillac." And the first thing I did with the bonus money I got from the Red Sox in 1967 was get her one.

But back in my salad days in high school, I was lucky to have anything that moved. Before my sister got married, she sometimes let me use her Studebaker Silver Hawk—the one I got pinched in at Savannah Beach that time. That was a fast little car, and I could have done all right racing it.

There were auto race tracks all over Georgia. Besides having fun, you could make a few bucks, but of course first you had to

83

have a car. If I hadn't been so busy with sports and nine-ball and school and all, I'd have bought a racing car as soon as I was old enough to get someone to sell me one.

My first car was a Chevy 245, fuel-injected and sharp-looking, but a pretty sick sonofagun on a race track. After I got beaten a few times, I made a deal with a guy who had a racing Corvette for sale. This was strictly for competition—it had never been on the street. He used to haul it to race tracks on a trailer.

The car wasn't any older than my 245, but it looked pretty beat up from racing. The Fiberglas was chipped and it didn't have much finish. You get enough of that drag-race dust on a car and you'll never get it off. But it could fly—handled right, you could make the price of it back in a couple of months. And when I was on my car-racing kick I really handled that thing right. I lost only about two races with it, while winning ten or twelve.

The only trouble with it was it ate gas and threw fan belts something awful. The damn thing only got about five miles to the gallon, and every time I drove it I knew I'd need two or three fan belts before I was through.

One time when we were broke, Betty Ann and I drove over to a fifty-buck winner-take-all race in Vidalia, about a hundred miles from Savannah. I knew every car in that race, and I could beat everyone. We left Savannah with a full tank of gas and eight bucks, so I didn't have any cushion— I *had* to beat them all or we'd never get home.

The races were short—only a quarter of a mile. I had to take it easy driving to Vidalia because I didn't want to have to buy any fan belts on the way over. Sure enough, she threw two while I was warming her up on the track, and I had to send somebody out to get a couple more—they cost seven bucks.

There were about three preliminaries and then the final, with cars competing from Alabama, Florida, and South Carolina, as well as Georgia. I knew everybody and all the cars—the same ones competed everywhere.

My first race was with a 1940 Ford with a Corvette engine in it. The car was old—this was 1958—but it had a hell of an engine. I beat him pretty good, then raced a 1957 Pontiac, the only car that scared me—because he had beaten me once. But I nosed him out by half a car length, then won a couple more races to get into the finals.

Now I was down to a quarter of a tank of gas, just enough for one last race, and one buck. I remember sitting on the starting line thinking, "If we don't win this one we'll have to thumb home." The only car that worried me was a new Chevy, but I guess he was just as worried about me because my times had been a tenth or two-tenths of a second better than his all night.

The flag went down and I was off like a shot. There wasn't anyone near me all the way around the track, and I won going away. I didn't find out until later what happened to the Chevy. He gave himself too much gas too soon and wasted three seconds just standing there burning rubber.

I got my prize in fifty one-dollar bills—that's how big-time those drag race promoters were—and I guess it was the first time Betty Ann and I felt comfortable in Vidalia. Our combined sighs of relief would have blown us back to Savannah. As it was, I could fill the tank, get another new fan belt, and drive home in style.

I raced cars here and there for a couple of years, thinking maybe someday I might throw baseball and everything else up and concentrate on auto racing until I won the Indianapolis 500. But I never got anywhere near Indianapolis. My racing career ended very suddenly on a little old country road about twenty-five miles out of Savannah. It was really just a county maintenance road, a seven-mile straightaway. Nobody ever used it, so we had informal drag races on it.

HAWK

One day I went out there in a Plymouth for a hundred-dollar match race against a guy in a Corvette. We put the dough up in advance and agreed that the guy in front would blink his lights when he was wide open, which was common practice in these informal races. We both figured we'd get up to 100 m.p.h. and anything over that depended on your nerve.

He got the jump on me, but I was right on his tail, the two of us going like hell. I glanced at my speedometer to see if we were up to 100, but the damn thing was broken, so all I could do was wait for his blinkers. When they went on I had a little left, jammed my foot to the floor and got ready to pass him. Just as I was about to swing out, I hit a bump and my car went straight up in the air. It landed on two wheels, and I had a hell of a time getting it settled on four. Even then, I fought the wheel to keep the car under control, and finally managed to pull it up to the side of the road. I leaned back and thought, "The hell with this. Let him have his hundred." Then I sat for ten or fifteen minutes, shaking as I thought of all the awful things that could have happened. When I calmed down enough to start the car, I drove the rest of the road like a farmer.

Later, the other guy told me he was going 140 miles an hour when I was right on his tail. I never raced again. And to this day I have never driven over 80.

Now, instead of speed, I go for looks. My pride and joy is a lavender dune buggy with velvet trimmings, a white rug about four inches thick, a bar, a refrigerator, a television set, and a record player. I bought it in Boston just before 1969 spring training, and I don't have the slightest idea how fast it will go. I've never opened it up and never will.

I've given up arm-wrestling, too. There was a time when I claimed the world's championship because nobody beat me for years. I arm-wrestled all over the place, for money, for drinks, or just for the hell of it, consistently beating guys bigger, stronger, and smarter.

More than strength, arm-wrestling requires psyching. You have to work yourself up to a pitch of excitement and desire, get your adrenalin running, convince yourself that you can beat the other guy, no matter how big and strong he looks. It's not really a sport so much as a stunt. Usually, if you're ready and right, the thing's all over in five seconds, although I've been in matches that lasted nearly a minute.

I guess I was maybe fifteen when I started arm-wrestling. When I beat everybody I was the pride of Savannah's arm-wrestling set. The guys around town used to bet as much as a hundred dollars on me whenever newcomers came around looking for matches, or when we went anywhere else.

We did most of our arm-wrestling in poolrooms, usually after settling up nine-ball matches. Everyone was relaxed and feeling good, and, when strangers were around, one of my pals would say, "We've got a guy here who can beat anyone arm-wrestling." Pretty soon they'd produce a guy, everybody would bet, and the match would be on.

Although I stood six-two, my present height, I looked like a pushover because I was so thin. I weighed around 170 in those days —I'm about 190 now—and there was always some big gorilla in the other gang who thought he could tear me apart. But I was unusually strong for my build, and my arms were so long that I generally had a reach advantage. Reach is very important in arm-wrestling. When you sit down opposite a guy whose arms are shorter than yours, you can get the jump on him because you have more leverage. And in arm-wrestling, the jump is everything.

One night after I came home from my second pro baseball season a few of us went up to Augusta for a little pool. We didn't have any kind of a formal circuit, but we played with groups from all over, sometimes in Savannah, sometimes elsewhere. The games lasted forever, often as long as sixteen hours. We knew our business so well that we seldom lost. I don't remember ever having gone to Augusta for nine-ball before. Somebody up there knew one of our guys and that was how we got together.

After we finished the pool game, we were sitting around having a bite to eat and something to drink before the long drive home, when one of their guys said, "Have you got anybody who can arm-wrestle?"

Billy DeLoach, one of my best friends, a real con man and a great guy, said, "Yeah, we've got a guy here who arm-wrestles every so often. Who have you guys got?"

There was a man behind the counter, broad-shouldered and stocky, with short blond hair, who looked as if he weighed maybe 220. He hadn't played pool with us because he just worked in the joint, serving sandwiches and soft drinks and stuff like that.

"This boy arm-wrestles," somebody said.

Billy hardly looked at him. He just pointed to me and said, "So does this one. What do you guys want to bet?"

Well, after seeing the lanky rail that I was in those days, the Augusta boys couldn't get their money down fast enough. I bet fifty on myself, and among the crowd we must have had four hundred bucks riding on me. Short, stocky 220-pounders were my meat, and I was sure I could beat this one.

But I nearly fainted when he came out from behind the counter. We didn't know he had been sitting on a stool and was about six inches taller than he looked—a giant of a guy, maybe six feet six and at least a hundred pounds heavier than I was. As he strolled out to the table where I sat, I thought, *Damn, Hawk, here's where you're gonna get your arm broken.*

Billy leaned over and whispered, "He's musclebound and his arms are shorter than yours. You can beat him. Just psych yourself and you'll be all right."

The Hawk astride Charley O. at Yankee Stadium. A great athlete he is; a jockey he's not. *Photo: Wide World*

Harrelson scores the winning run against the White Sox during Boston's drive for the Pennant in 1967. Duane Josephson is the Chicago catcher. *Photo: Wide World*

The fabled beach buggy. Beautiful. *Photo: Jerry Buckley*

Harrelson just after he was traded to Cleveland. The boots were made for walkin' but not quite yet. The Hawk retired shortly after this picture was taken. *Photo: Wide World*

The retirement was short-lived. Hawk agrees to play for Cleveland. Seated, Commissioner of Baseball Bowie Kuhn. Standing from left are: Gabe Paul, Cleveland President; Harrelson; his attorney, Robert Woolf; American League President Joe Cronin; Dick O'Connell, Boston Vice-President and General Manager. *Photo: Wide World*

It's raining on Hawk's arrival in Cleveland, but those may be rose-colored glasses. *Plain Dealer Photo, Richard J. Misch*

The only player in baseball who has his trademark on his uniform.
Photo: United Press International

The mustache is a phony, but everything else is *real*.
Photo: Jerry Buckley

So while this mammoth approached me I worked myself up into a peak—a real crescendo—and by the time he sat opposite me, I had myself all convinced. Billy stood there and said, "You ready, Hawk?"

"I'm ready."

"You ready?"

"Yeah," the other guy said, "I'm ready."

We put our elbows on the table, locked hands, and the minute Billy said, "Go!" I smashed his hand down on the table. It didn't take two seconds. Our guys let out a roar, picked up the dough, and walked out.

The biggest fellow I ever beat was a sailor at the Naval Air Station in Brunswick. We were over there playing pool, and just as we finished, this guy came in. He must have stood six-nine and weighed about 300, and he had a disposition like a lamb. A real, nice, friendly guy you couldn't help liking on sight. After we had been sitting around a while, he said, "I'll arm-wrestle anybody in the house for a beer." He wasn't bragging—just talking in a half-kidding way.

"Go ahead, Hawk, take him on," somebody said.

I psyched myself for a minute or two, then we went at it. That one didn't last five seconds because the sailor wasn't nearly as strong as he looked. After I got his hand down, he looked at me, grinned, and said, "Well, that makes you the champion of the air base."

I once arm-wrestled Duke Sims, now my teammate on the Cleveland Indians, who's about my height but heavier. We didn't have anything at stake—just wrestled for the hell of it. We put our elbows on the table, locked hands, and got going. Neither of us got a jump, and we strained for about ten seconds, and then the damn table collapsed. Later that night, I beat him after dinner in the restaurant where we ate.

One night at a baseball players' bowling tournament in Tampa

I was having a beer with Harmon Killebrew and Dick Stuart, who claimed to be the greatest arm-wrestler of all time. He was with the Red Sox then, one of the longest hitters and lousiest fielders in the league, and was always talking about his arm-wrestling.

I was still a fresh rookie—not even out of the minors yet—when I said, "Richard, I've heard all about your arm-wrestling, and I've got news for you. I can beat you."

"No, thanks," Stuart said. "I've retired. I'm making good money out of baseball and there's no sense hurting my arm."

"Hell," I said, "the way you play first base you don't need an arm."

I couldn't get him to arm-wrestle me and we never did find out which one of us was the champion. I kept going along, beating all comers for a couple of years, usually finishing guys off in ten seconds or less. Once in a while somebody would hold me to a draw, but I'd beat him eventually, so by the time I was in the big leagues I was pretty cocky about my arm-wrestling.

When I went up to the Athletics, I spent a lot of time around the Apartment Lounge, a real nice joint owned by a great guy and a wildly enthusiastic sports fan named Jack Haley. It was a hangout for all the Kansas City baseball and football players, and I got pretty friendly with some of the Chiefs, particularly Curt Merz and Bobby Hunt. One day Curt, who was six-four and weighed 265 pounds, happened to mention that he was a pretty good arm-wrestler. That was all I needed. Because it was the middle of the baseball season and I didn't want to hurt my arm, we agreed to go ten seconds, lay off if nobody won, then do the same thing over and over until one of us beat the other.

Well, after we started, we forgot all about the ten-second agreement. At that point, the two of us were still locked, each convinced he could beat the other. We kept on going—twenty, thirty, forty seconds—and I could feel myself weakening. At forty-five seconds he put me down, the first guy ever to beat me. We got up, walked over to the bar to get a drink, and my arm was so sore I couldn't lift the glass. I couldn't straighten it or throw a ball for three days.

When the baseball season ended, I tried Curt once more, but it was hopeless. He had beaten me once, and I couldn't get fired up. I sat there a full minute trying to psych myself. It was no good. He put me down in less than two seconds.

I never arm-wrestled again.

I mentioned sitting at the ballplayers' bowling tournament in Tampa with Killebrew and Stuart. By then I was a pretty good bowler, but I never had bowled in my life until I was seventeen. The year after my first season in baseball a couple of guys in bowling leagues around Savannah asked me to join them, but I said no. It seemed kind of a silly pastime to me until they got me to go out and watch them one night. I became intrigued after a while, and went off to an alley to try it. The next thing I knew, I was in up to my neck, partly because the pot games these guys played added up to a pretty good piece of change.

I got my own ball and shoes, and started in those pot games. A pot game is when eight or ten guys get together, each puts up twenty bucks or so, and the whole pot goes to the guy with the highest total at the end of the night. You could win three or four hundred bucks, and when I was hot none of the guys could beat me. I never shot a perfect game, but I often was up around 260 or 270. All you had to do to win a pot game was put a few of those together. I did that fairly regularly.

Sometimes, when we all had a little extra money, the pot got up into four figures. One night there was about fifteen hundred dollars riding on a pot game among about twenty-five of us. I started out hot, got a pretty good lead, and figured I was home. We played for hours and hours, and the longer we went the worse I got. We didn't quit until six in the morning—the owner kept the place open all night for us—and by then I had blown the whole works.

I never was so mad in my life. We lived near a marsh, and when

HAWK

I got home I thought, *It wasn't me—it was the damn ball.* I put the ball in a bag with my shoes, went out to the marsh, swung the bag around my head like a hammer thrower, and tossed it as far as I could.

When I thought about it the next day, I decided I'd been nuts. Since I knew about where the bag had landed, I went out looking for it. But that marsh was awfully gooey, and once the bag had sunk it was gone. I had to buy new shoes and a new ball.

The last time I bowled for heavy money, I won a bundle just at the right time. Betty Ann and I had been married about six months and, as usual, were lovey-dovey one day and at each other's throats the next. We both wanted to get away from Savannah and thought maybe Michigan, where my sister lived, would be great. She lived in Monroe, about twenty-five miles from Detroit. She and Betty Ann got along very well, and she had been after us to go up there. Neither of us had ever seen Detroit, which gave us another incentive to go.

The damn trouble was, we couldn't afford a trip to Jacksonville, much less Monroe, Michigan. Well, one night I got into a pot game about eight o'clock. It ended at eleven, when most of the boys had to go home, but one guy, a good friend of mine who liked to play for high stakes, was still around.

"How about a few games at a hundred bucks each?" he said.

That was all right with me, although I didn't have twenty bucks to my name. It turned out he didn't have that much cash with him either, but I didn't know it at the time. We started playing and I caught fire. When the guy had 150 I had 157, when he had 160 I had 162—it was that kind of night. And when I slipped he slipped. Once I had 127 or something and he had 125. Finally, when he owed me eleven hundred dollars, he said, "The hell with it. Let's quit."

He wrote a check for eleven hundred and handed it to me. I rarely took checks and then usually held them in case we played again and I lost. But this time I needed the money to go to Michigan, so I said, "Is the check good right now?"

"You're damn right it's good right now," he said.

I cashed it the next day, and that was how Betty Ann and I got up to Michigan to see Iris. Except for a fight with a guy who whistled at Iris in a steak house in Detroit—she was eight months pregnant and big as a house—it was a hell of a trip.

I do pretty well staying out of fights now, but it took me a long time to learn. The last one was in Washington while I was with the Senators, just before spring training in 1967. I was having a few drinks with Steve Thurlow and Jimmy Carroll of the Redskins in a place called Sonny's one Friday night. The joint was crowded —really jam packed—and you couldn't move. We were sitting at a table, practically rubbing elbows with the people at the tables around us.

There were three guys and a girl at the table nearest me. When one of the guys spilled some beer on his pants, the girl leaned over and said, "Do you have a handkerchief?"

"Certainly," I said, and passed one over to her. She gave it to the guy, and when he finished wiping himself off he handed it back to her and she offered it back to me.

"Tell him he can keep it," I said.

She leaned over to speak to him, and I heard him say, "Tell him to take his handkerchief and shove it," specifying where I could shove it.

Very casually the girl turned back to me and repeated exactly what he had said, word for word, including the vulgarity. I blew my stack. I went over to the guy and, when he stood up to meet me, I punched him in the face.

The next thing I knew somebody broke a beer bottle over my head—I knew it was a beer bottle because I had been hit by beer bottles before—and somebody else jumped me and held me down. By this time Steve Thurlow and Jimmy Carroll, neither of whom knew what the hell was happening except that I was in trouble, had jumped across the table and started throwing punches, and the joint was in an uproar.

I was bleeding like a stuck pig, but all I remember was that a beautiful new mustard-and-red-colored sweater I had just bought was being ruined by all the blood. Pretty soon the cops came, and they took me to the hospital to sew me up—ten stitches, three on top of my head and seven behind my ear. The stitches were still in when I showed up at Pompano Beach for spring training.

I swore off fights then, and haven't been in one since. Believe me, I'm going to have to be out of my mind to get messed up in another.

One of the few sports that never appealed to me was tennis. The only time I played was my first year in baseball, when Steve Kelly, a ballplayer who once came close to junior national ranking, got me out on a court with him. I didn't even know how to hold a tennis racket properly. After he showed me, we started playing, and he murdered me a couple of sets. Then I began to get the hang of it and, although Kelly continued to beat me, he was obviously weakening. We must have played about ten sets by then, but I still felt pretty good, while he was running around with his tongue hanging out.

"Come on," he said. "Let's quit."

"Quit, hell," I said. "I'm just getting warmed up."

"I can hardly lift my racket."

"Just one more set," I said.

I killed him. I was a lot stronger anyhow, and he was completely pooped. I think he won one game and I beat him, 6–1.

Man, was he red-ass!

"Damn you," he yelled. "You're not supposed to beat me the first time you ever play the game. I'm a hell of a tennis player."

"It's a lousy game," I said. "Too easy."

7 | Learning the Business

If I had had my choice of professional sports, I probably would have picked basketball. Actually, it was my best sport all through high school, and I made the All-American schoolboy team my senior year. But at six feet two, I wasn't big enough for the pros.

Not that I didn't like baseball. Although it wasn't my favorite sport, I enjoyed it and always found time for it. I really didn't know what the hell I was, because I played everywhere. I liked the outfield and first base, but I was all over the infield, and pitched and caught, too, both in high school and Junior Legion ball. We were the Legion state champs, and a dozen scouts followed us wherever we played. I wasn't the only one who interested them. They were looking at four or five of us.

They couldn't make any offers before I graduated from high school, but they could talk to me, and many of them did. The only ones I got to know well were Clyde Kluttz of the Athletics, Ray Hayworth of the Cubs, and Leon Hamilton of the Dodgers. The Indians, the Phillies, and the Tigers also talked to me, but weren't so hot after me as the others.

I had the build and the power of a good right-handed hitter, I was fast and I had a strong arm. Those are the ingredients every scout looks for. My fielding, although unorthodox, was deceptively good. Everyone laughs today at the way I catch the ball one-handed. I was doing it then, too, which I guess appalled the scouts, but none of them wanted me for my fielding. I could hit the hell out of the ball, and they knew that was something I was born with. They figured I could be taught to field.

Cleveland wanted to sign me as a pitcher. You know how it is with kids—the best hitter is usually the best pitcher, too. A Cleveland scout saw me pitch a one-hitter at Benedictine, and I guess I pitched a few Legion games. I really didn't know how to pitch. All I had was a good fast ball and a dinky curve, which I hardly used. I usually went through a whole ball game throwing nothing but the fast ball.

Hayworth, who was once a catcher himself, recommended me to the Cubs as a catcher. He happened to see me do just about all the catching I ever did—thirty-nine games for the Legion club one year. The regular catcher was the son of an Air Force officer who was transferred, so I filled in for him.

I did a hell of a job, if I say so myself. I knew instinctively how to call a game and wasn't afraid to throw the ball around. The kids couldn't steal on me, and every so often I picked somebody off. The trouble was, I got awfully tired squatting behind the plate wearing all that heavy gear. I did fine for about twenty games, but after that I couldn't move. The plate umpires cursed me to high heaven because I just didn't bother to reach for wild pitches when nobody was on base, and they had to chase the ball down.

Still, Hayworth thought I had a hell of a future as a catcher. He said when I was older and had filled out and got used to catching I wouldn't tire so easily, but I didn't like the damn job—it was too much work. I couldn't see myself spending long hot summers behind the plate.

Oh, I wouldn't mind a game here and there. As a matter of fact, I volunteered to catch for the Red Sox when it looked as if they'd be in trouble for receivers early in the 1968 season. Elston Howard had a bad arm and the only other catcher we had was Russ Gibson. I told Manager Dick Williams I'd catch if Gibby got hurt, but I guess Dick didn't want to take any chances because the club brought Russ Nixon up from the minors as a back-up catcher the next day.

I cried a little over that. I would have liked to catch a big-league ball game. I'll bet I could still call a hell of a game, throw guys out on the bases, and keep the ball in front of me all the time. I don't know how I'd do with pop fouls, but with that great big mitt I don't see how I could miss many of them.

Of all the scouts I met, the one I liked best was Clyde Kluttz. He came to the house from time to time, pointed out the advantages of going to Kansas City, and said the Athletics would give me a sizable bonus. We didn't talk specific figures. Most of Kluttz's argument was that I'd move up faster with the Athletics, which was true. They needed so much help that a kid really did have a better opportunity with them than with anyone else.

After I graduated, they offered me a good bonus, spread out over a three-year period. The only club that offered more was the Dodgers, but I couldn't see signing with them. This was 1959, when they were loaded with power. It would have taken a kid like me six years to get out from under their ponderous minor-league setup.

I signed with the Athletics on June 6, right after my high-school graduation, and was ordered to Olean, New York, in the Class D New York–Penn League. I took my time reporting—in fact, I didn't want to go there at all. I stalled around home as long as I could get away with it, and finally joined the Olean club about the first of July.

In the meantime, I went car crazy. First I bought the Pontiac for my mama. Then I got myself a Corvette, kept it a few days, turned it in for another Corvette, didn't like that one either and ended up with a Cadillac—all in the space of a week and a half.

Brains? I must have thrown mine into the marsh with my bowling ball that time.

Olean was dull as hell, the other towns in the league duller, and the living conditions strictly bush. We stayed in rooming houses, traveled by bus, and ate in greasy spoons all over the circuit. Robby Robertson, the manager, put me in the outfield, where I didn't exactly knock anybody dead. I made three errors and batted .192 in forty-three games, but I hit eight home runs and most of them went ten miles. Just before the season ended, Robby told me if I really worked at it, I could make it to the majors because I had all the equipment.

"But you've really got to work at it," he said. "This isn't an easy game or just a fun game. You're in the pros now."

Glad to be home, I forgot baseball for the winter, then reported to the Sanford club of the Class D Florida State League in 1960. That was my first spring training, and I had a ball. Robby managed there that year, and kept after me to bust my butt instead of taking life easy, the way I had at Olean. I played first base, really did work hard, and it paid off. In the first half of the season I led the league in batting and home runs and was second in RBIs—hit .356, had nine homers, and drove in fifty-six runs. It looked as if I was off to the races.

I looked forward to the second half of the season, but about a week after it started I began to lose weight so fast it was obvious there was something seriously wrong. I didn't feel sick, but when I dropped twenty-two pounds in three days, I was put in hospital isolation. After some preliminary tests, the doctors thought I had leukemia, although I didn't find that out until later. I wasn't scared until my mama showed up, saying she had been sent for. Only then did I think I was going to cash in my chips.

I was kept in the hospital almost a month before the doctors decided that all I had was German measles. I was still underweight when I reported back to the ball club, and of course my season was ruined. I had only one more home run, drove in about thirteen more runs, and ended up with an anemic .227 batting average.

If it hadn't been for that damn illness I might have made it to Class A in 1961, but instead I went to Visalia in the Class C California League. I had a real good season there under Bobby Hofman, the manager, who played me at first base, third base, and the outfield. The Athletics still didn't know where I belonged, and I'm sure he had instructions to try everything he could think of.

I played practically every game and, while my fielding was nothing to brag about, I had a great year at the plate—twenty-five home runs, one hundred fourteen RBIs and a .301 batting average. Hofman kept after me to use two hands fielding, but I was more comfortable using one, especially at first base, where you have to do so much stretching. Since I played eighty-four games there and figured that would be my regular position, I didn't see much sense trying to become a two-handed artist instead of a one-handed journeyman.

Bobby was strictly experimenting when he put me at third. I had to use two hands there, of course, but I did most of my fielding with my chest. Every time one of those hot shots came down my way, I just let it hit me, then picked it up and threw to first. But a third baseman I definitely wasn't, and I never would have been a good one.

Although I played a few games in the outfield at Binghamton in the Class A Eastern League in 1962, I was primarily the first baseman. Granny Hamner was the manager, and he helped me through the greatest season I ever had in the minors. I played in every game and led the league's first basemen in fielding—yes, in fielding.

No one in the world could call me a modest man, and I'll prove it right now by telling you I'm one hell of a first baseman. That year at Binghamton removed all the doubts I might ever have had, and I still have no doubts about it. With the exception of George Scott who was shifted from first base to third by the Red Sox this year,

I'm the best fielding—that's right, fielding—first baseman in the American League right now.

I also had a great year at the plate in Binghamton—in fact, set records in homers and runs-batted-in that I don't think have been broken yet. I had thirty-eight home runs and a hundred thirty-eight RBIs to go with a .272 batting average.

Hamner was a great guy to play for, tough as hell, but he knew how to handle young ballplayers. One of the original Whiz Kids who won the 1950 pennant for the Phillies, he made you hustle every minute and fined you if you didn't. He was particularly impatient with cry babies who were always claiming sore arms or something to get a day off. And if a pitcher getting clobbered began claiming arm trouble, Granny made him stay in and take his lumps.

Many minor-league managers tend to pamper kids, fining them one day and telling them to forget it the next. Not Hamner. He hit you with a bundle, and it stuck. The year I was with him he didn't give anyone back a dime.

We had Lew Krausse, Jr., that year. Krausse, whose old man was a scout and a former big leaguer, had collected something like a hundred-twenty-five-thousand-dollar bonus, then made one of the most sensational professional baseball debuts in history. The Athletics brought him right up from high school, and the first game he pitched was a three-hit shutout over the Angels.

Only eighteen at the time, Lew spent the rest of the 1961 season at Kansas City, but obviously wasn't ready for the majors. They sent him to Binghamton, where he and I recognized each other as kindred souls and became buddies almost on sight. We both liked to raise a little hell and we both contributed small amounts to Hamner's fine kitty from time to time.

Granny understood kids and I'm sure got a lot of secret laughs out of the foolish boys-will-be-boys shenanigans we were always trying to get away with. But one thing he wouldn't tolerate was disobedience on the ballfield. What you did wrong off the field might be worth only a few bucks in fines, but if you broke a rule on the field it cost you real money.

Krausse learned that one night when he refused to wait for a relief pitcher before leaving the mound. This was one of Hamner's strictest regulations. No pitcher was ever to leave until his relief arrived. Lew, who had a terrible temper, blew his stack when the opposition started getting to him. We had a three- or four-run lead, and when it was obvious Lew couldn't hold it, Granny went to the mound to pull him out. Instead of waiting, Lew stormed off, went to the clubhouse, showered, and left the ball park.

Hamner didn't say a word that night, but the next day he fined Krausse five hundred dollars. When Lew heard about it, he raised such a stink that Granny added another two-fifty. A seven-hundred-fifty-dollar fine is a big one in the major leagues. In the minors, it's a catastrophe for most guys. Of course, Granny knew Krausse could afford it, but he wouldn't have let any pitcher get away with what Lew had done. I'm sure he would have fined the most poverty-stricken guy on the club a hundred at least.

When I was with Binghamton I nearly threw my arm out learning to smoke. Krausse and I were under the stands practicing inhaling when I heard over the loud-speaker, "Ken Harrelson, report to center field for the throwing contest." I'd forgotten all about the damn throwing contest, a feature of the evening to help attract customers to the game at Elmira, where we were playing that night.

A little dizzy from the inhaling, I threw down my cigarette, ran out to center field, and without a single warmup, threw the ball as far as I could. I felt something go *blip* in my arm and it hurt like hell. I couldn't throw for a week, and was lucky I didn't ruin my whole career. All I succeeded in doing that night was acquire the cigarette habit. I still have it.

I got along great with Hamner. He was the first manager I ever had who had spent much time in the major leagues, and he taught me a lot about what to expect there. He helped me particularly with my hitting. He was the first to tell me how big-league pitchers use patterns to set up hitters, and he taught me a lot about how certain situations are handled.

He talked a lot about concentration. He was the first manager I ever had point out its importance. He kept telling me I was a sure big-league slugger if I concentrated properly at the plate. He told me that nobody standing there could afford to let his mind wander for an instant. To this day, I deliberately make mine a complete blank except for the guy out there on the mound and the ball in his hand.

I always had good concentration in sports. Golf and baseball are the two that most require absolute concentration. While natural ability and desire are essential, it is concentration that gets you to the top.

I've never seen a man in any sport with better concentration than Carl Yastrzemski of the Red Sox. He starts psyching himself on the bench before he even starts for the on-deck circle. By the time he gets there, his mind is clear of every thought except the opposing pitcher. As he crouches, he never takes his eyes off the man or the ball after it leaves his hand. That concentration is so intense that Yaz walks to the plate automatically when his turn comes. Except to get himself set there, look down the line in case a coach has a signal for him, and touch all parts of the plate with the bat to be sure he's covering it, I don't think his eyes ever leave the pitcher.

This is why Yaz is such a great hitter and will be as long as he plays ball. I know of few great hitters—there may be a couple here and there—who don't put concentration first on the list of prerequisites for success at the plate. Obviously, an outstanding hitter must have the mechanical equipment and the natural ability. That goes without saying. But outside of those factors, the difference between real greatness and just-average success is his power of concentration.

While Hamner was the first to talk concentration to me, the man who made me understand it was Al Dark when I played for him at Kansas City. He did it by comparing hitting to golf, a game that demands absolute concentration. Dark could make me relate baseball to golf, and a coach who could do that could help me out of slumps better than one who couldn't.

Yaz, for example, not being a good golfer, couldn't help me out of slumps as easily as Dark could, or Al Vincent, the Athletics' batting coach when I was at Kansas City, or Bobby Doerr, the Red Sox batting coach. Vincent and Doerr are both golfers, and when they talked in terms of golf they were talking my language.

By using golf principles, Vincent got me out of a habit that would have ruined me if I hadn't broken it. I had a tendency to jump the ball—stride too soon so that my head was moving forward as the pitch was coming in.

"When you swing at a golf ball your head must be perfectly still," he used to say. "And the same thing is true in baseball. The ball is coming in at ninety or a hundred miles an hour. If you move your head it seems to be coming even faster. Watch any great hitter—I don't care who—and you'll notice that his head stays in the same position as he follows through, and only then does he move it."

"In golf," Al told me, "you must keep your head behind the ball. And it's the same thing in baseball. The swing is different. In one case, you're always hitting down and at a stationary target. In the other, you're also hitting down but at a moving target. In both cases, the more hands and less body you put into your swing, the more likely you are to hit the ball squarely."

Bobby Doerr talked the same way when I was with the Red Sox. Whenever I went into a slump, he told me, "You've got to stay behind the ball, you've got to keep your head still, you've got to follow the ball all the way with your eyes. And after you hit the ball, keep your head down, keep it still—just as in golf."

103

Thus, golf helps me in baseball, as it helps any golfing ballplayer. I learned a long time ago that I can't play golf during the baseball season—partly because it bothers my concentration and partly because of the difference in the swing. Good-hitting ballplayers who don't play golf are at a disadvantage in the one respect that they can't relate the two games. I can.

Ted Williams, probably the greatest teacher of hitting who ever lived, can't help me as much as he helps others because he's not a golfer. I can listen to Williams talk hitting all day. He has his own ideas, knows how to express them, and is absolutely great on the subject. But for me, he is more interesting than helpful. When I'm in a slump, I can get more out of a session with Dark, Doerr, or Vincent than I can with Williams. If this smacks a bit of treason, I don't mean it to. I'm one of Ted's most ardent admirers.

It's funny, but while golf helps me in baseball, baseball doesn't help me in the least in golf. I think golf is the tougher of the two games. They're both more pressure than action games, but in baseball you have company. There are eight other guys on the same side with you. You're trying to help them and they're trying to help you.

But golf is like boxing. You're all alone. Nobody can help you, nobody can swing the club for you, nobody can keep your nerves under control. Like that time it took me so long to hit the dinky little wedge shot at Miami Springs. Everything depended on that shot, and the longer I stood there the more I realized it. That's real pressure—the worst kind of pressure in sports.

Baseball pressure is tough enough, but it isn't that tough. Don't get me wrong—it's no pushover. You can play nine innings in the outfield, not handle a single chance, yet be a nervous wreck at the finish. The reason is that, even though you never have a chance, you always have to expect one. You can relax only between pitches. Once the ball leaves the pitcher's hand, you must be tense and ready.

But if I have my choice of waiting for a key baseball chance to come my way in a World Series or having the National Open riding on a fifteen-foot putt on the eighteenth green, I'll take the World Series. They're both nerve-racking. But that fifteen-foot putt is all up to me. And the chances of my having to handle the ball in the World Series are eight-to-one against.

Those aren't bad odds.

8 | Baseball, Poker, and Laughs

My first spring training with the Athletics, at Bradenton, Florida, was 1963. I was a hot-shot twenty-one-year-old kid fresh off that fantastic season at Binghamton, where my thirty-eight homers and a hundred and thirty-eight RBIs had broken the Eastern League record. I swaggered into that ball park in Bradenton ready to bet my salary that I'd be the biggest thing Kansas City baseball had seen since Mickey Mantle played there when it was in the American Association.

The Athletics manager of the moment was Eddie Lopat, one of a long string of guys hired and fired by Charley Finley, the club's colorful owner. The mortality rate of big-league managers is high. Finley's was astronomical. In nine years he had nine managers, counting Hank Bauer, whom he hired twice, as two. I played for five of the nine without putting two full seasons back-to-back with the ball club.

Lopat was a wonderful guy, but only a fair manager. He was too nice to get mad, had trouble handling some of the guys, and wasn't sure how to run a ball game. I loved him because he was always great to me, but, like everybody else, I walked all over him. None of us bothered with such little annoyances as curfews

107

and training rules, but Eddie didn't mind. He never fined me for breaking them, and if he fined anybody else I didn't hear about it.

Our coaches were Jimmy Dykes, Mel McGaha, and Gus Niarhos. Dykes, a veteran of a million years in the majors, was as easygoing as Lopat. Niarhos, the bullpen catcher, had his own chores and never worked with the infielders. But McGaha, a former Cleveland manager and later one of Finley's, was a hard-working, no-nonsense guy, tall, sharp, and tough. He had once been one of the roughest players in the National Basketball Association, a hatchet man for the New York Knickerbockers. He liked Lopat personally, but took a very dim view of Eddie's lackadaisical managerial methods.

Tough as he was, I respected and liked McGaha, who helped me no end. Since I was a fun-loving rover, I needed that type of guy to keep after me, eat me out for foolish mistakes, and make me understand that nothing I had ever done at Binghamton was going to help me at Kansas City.

Although cocky, I was really pretty nervous starting out. It may only have been the Athletics, one of the worst teams in baseball at the time, but it was still the big leagues. Every rookie, no matter how good he thinks he is, dies a million deaths during his first spring training with a major-league club. Besides working his brains out, he's scared to death of being cut. And after the first three weeks, the ax is always hanging over his head because every club must get down to twenty-five players by opening day.

I hit the hell out of the ball, and thought sure I had it made, in spite of the fact that there were days when I played first base like a clod. After all, the Athletics weren't so powerful that they could afford to dump a long-hitting right-hander, no matter how lousy his fielding. Anyhow, now that I think about it, my fielding wasn't that bad.

Except for one day in Fort Lauderdale, where we played the Yankees in their new ball park. In those days the Yankees were still great, and the prospect of facing them for the first time was a little hairy even to an egocentric like me. They still had Mantle and Roger Maris and Yogi Berra and Bobby Richardson and Elston Howard and all those guys. Joe DiMaggio was always there for spring training. During games he sat in a little cage behind the first-base coach's box. I tell you, for a kid to see these guys and play this ball club for the first time, even in an exhibition game, was enough to cause goose-pimples.

If I ever wanted to make a big impression, that was the day. I'd show these great Yankees a thing or two. And I'd show that Joe DiMaggio something. Since he'd be practically on top of me, he'd know what a hell of a ballplayer I was. He found out that day all right.

Richardson, the Yankees' leadoff man, hit an easy bounder down the first-base line. As I reached for it, it caromed off my knee for an error. Tresh flied out or something, then Maris came up. He hit a hard ground ball down the first-base line which went right between my legs for another error. Up came Mantle, and he hit a hot shot which would have been a double-play ball if it hadn't bounced off my chest for a third error.

By this time, the whole ball park was rocking with laughter. DiMaggio screamed gags at me between hee-haws. I could see the Yankees roaring in their dugout behind first base, with Berra actually rolling around the bench, holding his sides. Over on our bench Lopat was laughing so hard he was crying and wiping his face with a towel.

I didn't know whether to laugh or cry until Eddie Hurley, the first-base umpire, said, "O.K., Hawk. You've filled the bases. Now you've got them where you want them."

Then I broke up along with everyone else.

Joe Pepitone, the next hitter, hit one to my left. When it skittered off my glove for another error that let in a run and kept the bases full, I was in shock. Which, I suppose, was why I forgot to cover first base on the next play. Somebody hit a ball down the third-base line, where Ed Charles made a great stop and a perfect throw. The ball flew into right field and a couple more runs streamed in.

Now the Yankees had three runs and two men still on base, all because of me. Five errors—four that counted and one of omission —had accounted for the works, and everyone in the ball park was roaring. On the Yankee bench, guys were hanging on to each other, and when I looked at ours, the first one I saw was Lopat, his glasses in one hand and his head between his legs, while his shoulders were shaking. And everyone else, it seemed, was having just as good a time.

Even John O'Donoghue, our pitcher, who had been sore as hell at first, was wiping his eyes, laughing so hard he couldn't pitch. When he walked a guy, somebody said, "See? Harrelson isn't the only guy who can fill the bases," and I broke up again. The next guy up hit a grand slam home run. Somehow or other, that didn't seem so funny, but before things got too serious, I managed to provide one more laugh.

With two out, somebody hit a soft liner right at me, and I nearly loused even that up. The ball popped out of my glove, landing two feet from the bag. As I reached for it, I fell on all fours, then crawled on hands and knees to beat the runner to the bag. I just lay there for a minute, laughing so hard I couldn't get up. And when I finally did and ran across the field to our bench, the whole park sounded like a Minsky's audience.

When I went to bat I got a standing ovation. I lifted my cap and bowed half a dozen times, making a complete circle so I wouldn't miss anybody. Then I hit into a double play.

Lopat didn't say a word to me, but the next morning he sent me to Tampa with the B team to play the Reds' B club. We all headed for the back of the bus—ballplayers always head for the back of the bus to get as far away from the manager as possible—

but I didn't stay there long. McGaha was acting manager of the B team, and he made me go up and sit with him. Believe me, I wasn't happy. Mel is a stern man, and I knew exactly what he wanted to talk to me about.

"Hawk, I suppose you thought you were pretty funny yesterday," he said.

I hemmed and hawed, and McGaha said, "Well, I didn't think you were funny. If I had been managing that club, I'd have hauled your ass out of there the first time you cracked a smile. You better not pull anything like that today."

He ate me out all the way to Tampa, and when we arrived at the ball park—we had dressed in Bradenton—he said, "Don't go into the locker room. Go right to the field."

When I got there, McGaha put me on first base and started drilling balls at me. He ran me ragged, hitting line drives, pop flies, ground balls, to my right, to my left, right at me, everywhere. He made me run toward the plate to field bunts, and then throw to first, and he made me field grounders, throw them to second, then get back to first in time to complete imaginary double plays.

Just before letting me go he said, "You want to be a ballplayer, maybe you'll make this club. You want to be a clown, go get a job in the circus."

Although I liked to have fun even in ball games, I realized then there was a time and place for everything, and I had picked the wrong time at the wrong place. From then on, I worked like hell and had a great spring training. I hurt my ankle sliding into second base one day, but it wasn't serious enough to keep me out of the lineup, and I thought surely I had it made.

I didn't. Before breaking camp, the Athletics assigned me to Portland in the Pacific Coast League. That teed me off good, but there wasn't anything I could do about it except pack my wife and daughter into the car and head for the West Coast. I wasn't the only one cut. By the time the season began, about half the guys on the Portland club were kids I had either played with somewhere else or who had been in Bradenton with me.

The Portland manager was a nice guy named Les Peden, who apparently had instructions to try me in the outfield, because that was where he played me most of the time. When I was up there at the plate, it didn't matter where I played, because I just hammered the hell out of the ball the first month of the season. After thirty-seven ball games I was way over .300 and led the league with nine homers and thirty-one RBIs. With ballplayers shuttling back and forth between Kansas City and Portland, I thought sure I'd be called up any minute, but nothing happened. As other guys who weren't doing half as well went to the big club I thought, *What the hell do they expect me to do? I'm the hottest hitter in the Pacific Coast League and they're letting me rot here.* It wasn't long before the hottest hitter in the Pacific Coast League was also the maddest.

Then I went into a terrible slump—couldn't buy a hit, no matter who was pitching. One night in Seattle Jerry Stephenson struck me out four times in a row, making me 0 for 14. My batting average dropped to exactly .300 and my spirits to zero. When the same pitcher could fan me four times in one night I was in a bad way. And if the Athletics wouldn't call me up when I was murdering the ball, how could I expect them to send for me when I was everybody's patsy?

I felt so low that I did something I seldom do—got into a poker game. I'm a pretty good poker player, but it always seemed to me sort of a stupid way to lose money. I'd rather depend on brains, muscle, or athletic skill than the luck you need in a card game. Since that night, I've played poker very rarely.

The last time was in Gus Niarhos's room at the Leamington Hotel in Minneapolis while I was with the Athletics. Gus, normally a sweet guy, was nervous and high strung, and had a terrible temper, especially when he was worried about anything. During the baseball season he always had plenty to worry about, because he was petrified every time he had to fly, and we flew everywhere.

Niarhos was so bad he practically had to be led by the nose onto an airplane. Some of the guys made things worse by predicting all kinds of disasters. When he was in earshot they'd say there was a big storm ahead, or the struts on the wings didn't seem very secure, or the pilot wasn't sure where he was, and Gus would go crazy.

This particular night the plane picking us up was so late getting into Minneapolis that we had four or five hours to kill in our rooms. As usual when he knew he'd have to fly, Gus was very nervous. We were playing dealer's choice—draw or, mostly, five- or seven-card stud—Gus, Moe Drabowski, Jerry Lumpe, Norm Siebern, and me.

We weren't playing for much—a buck ante, small bets, and limited raises. The most a guy could lose in one sitting was maybe fifty bucks. Besides being jumpy over the plane flight, Gus was losing, which just got him more agitated. Drabowski, who was a very good card player, was dealing "jack's trips," a draw game in which it takes jacks or better to open and at least three of a kind to win. Since you often had to ante four or five times before you got a winner, the pot could get big pretty fast.

We were on about the sixth round of a jack's-trips game when Drabowski, who was dealing, counted the pot and it was a dollar short.

"Gus, you didn't ante," Moe said.

"You're crazy, Moe," Gus said. "I anted."

"Well, let's all ante again," Moe said.

So we all anted again. There must have been thirty-five dollars—mostly ones—in the pot. Gus was fuming because he thought Moe was calling him a liar, and Moe knew it. As he was dealing, Moe said, "Now, Gus, don't get teed off, because I know you didn't ante the last time."

Gus looked at Moe, stood up, grabbed all the money on the

table, took it into the bathroom and flushed it down the john. Then he came back and said, "Now we'll all ante again and we'll know it this time."

I haven't played poker since.

Anyhow, that night Stephenson struck me out four times in Seattle, I got into a poker game after we got back from the ball park around eleven o'clock. Drabowski was in that game, too, along with Paul Seitz and Virgil Bernhardt, a couple of guys who never made it to the majors for more than a cup of coffee, if that.

Drabowski was killing us all at first, but around four o'clock I started winning and was nearly even when the phone rang. That must have been about six or six-thirty in the morning.

It was Pat Friday, the Athletics' general manager.

"Do you want to play for Kansas City?" he said.

"Sure," I said. "When do you want me there?"

"We've got a game at Chicago tonight. Catch a plane and you might be able to get there in time to suit up."

Bleary-eyed, I packed and headed for the airport. I just had time to call Betty Ann in Portland before getting a Denver plane with a connection for Chicago. Betty Ann was a little upset. Although I had been with five teams in five years, this was the first time I had ever switched in mid-season. I told her to sit tight. Even though I wasn't too well acquainted with Charley Finley yet, I had already seen enough of his shuffling around to know I might be back in Portland any time.

As a matter of fact, I couldn't understand why the Athletics called me up when they did. When I was hitting the hell out of the ball they ignored me. They waited for me to go into the worst slump of my career before sending for me.

So help me, I didn't think I'd ever make it. The trip from Portland to Denver was all right, but from Denver to Chicago was a nightmare. We started off in heavy weather and it got worse as we went along. Never in my life have I seen an airplane pitch and toss and dip and tumble the way this one did. It was the middle of the day, but you'd never know it. It was so dark out we couldn't see the wings except when lightning flashed, which happened every few seconds. After a while I didn't dare look out the window because the wings were quivering and dipping at twenty-degree angles. I couldn't stand the thought of seeing one of them drop off, which I was sure would happen.

Since the plane was nearly empty, the two stewardesses didn't have much to do. I sat in the very last seat with one arm around each, consoling them while they cried from sheer fright. One had been flying four years. The other, who had been around only a year or so, was too frightened to talk. Neither had ever seen anything like it.

They had company—me. More scared than I had ever been in my life, I was so sure we'd crash that I gave up any thought of making it to Chicago. I remember thinking all through the flight, *Damn—you finally get a chance to play in the big leagues and you're not even going to get there.* I could just see the headlines: DENVER–CHICAGO PLANE CRASHES. And in little type, listing the dead: "K. Harrelson, Savannah. Baseball player."

That's all the ink I'd get. Outside of Betty Ann and our little girl and my mama and my sister, nobody would give a damn.

I have crisscrossed the country by air God knows how many times since and I've been through some rough storms, but never one like that. Whenever we run into a little turbulence, guys start comparing it to other wild trips, but I'll stack mine against any of them. I don't know how we got through it. All I know is that when we landed in Chicago, I wobbled out so glad to be alive that I didn't care whether I'd make it to the ball park or not. I ran into one of the stewardesses on a flight to the West Coast about two years later, and she said, "That was still my worst trip." Mine, too.

When I arrived at the ball park, Lopat said, "You're just pinch-hitting for a while, but don't worry. We'll give you plenty of chance to play."

Dead tired from playing cards all night, still shaking from that horrible plane trip from Denver, I was in no shape to do anything but sleep. They gave me a uniform, and I worked out before the game, then sat on the bench, hoping Lopat wouldn't need me. But Juan Pizarro, pitching for the White Sox, had us beaten, and Lopat sent me up to pinch-hit in the ninth. I struck out on three pitches I didn't even see.

In Minnesota for a series with the Twins, I sat out the first game. The next day Jim Kaat, a tough left-hander, was the Twins pitcher, and Lopat started me on first base. I got my first big-league hit, a single, my first time up. Later we piled up a pretty good lead. I went out three times, and when I came up in the ninth Bill Pleis was pitching for the Twins.

Before I moved to the on-deck circle, Lopat said, "Don't hit anything but a slider. He'll throw a lot of fast balls, but if you wait long enough you'll see the slider, and his is lousy. Just wait for it."

I waited while Pleis threw five straight fast balls, two for strikes. Now the count was three and two, and I knew I'd have to swing at the next pitch, no matter what it was, if it came into the strike zone. Sure enough, it was a slider, and I belted it into the left center-field seats. That gave me two for five, including a home run, in my first complete major-league ball game.

Norm Siebern was the regular first baseman, and I played less there than in the outfield. While I didn't knock anybody dead, I didn't do badly. In a total of seventy-nine games I hit six homers, knocked in twenty-three runs, batted .230, and collected a thousand splinters on my fanny sitting on the bench. I got into many games only as a pinch-hitter or fill-in outfielder.

Watching Eddie Lopat manage was an education in futility. Although he knew baseball—witness his advice to me to hit only

Pleis's slider—he couldn't run a ball game. I guess he tried to keep everything in his head instead of writing it down, because he never remembered who had played and who hadn't. By not thinking ahead, he often ran out of the ballplayers he needed most.

One night when we were losing by about three runs in the seventh with the pitcher scheduled to lead off, Lopat sent Turk Alusik up to pinch-hit. Alusik was having a hell of a year—hitting around .470 as a pinch-hitter and maybe the best clutch man in the league. He doubled, then scored when somebody else singled.

After scoring, Turk went into the runway between the bench and the locker room to have a smoke. He was still there when the other team brought in a southpaw to pitch to one of our left-handed hitters who was hopeless against left-handed pitching. Lopat yanked him and yelled, "Alusik, go up there and hit." When nothing happened, Eddie went crazy.

"Turk, for crissake, get a bat—get a bat and hit," Lopat yelled. He walked up and down the bench, howling, "Where's Turk? Where's Turk? He's gotta get up there."

Turk, still smoking in the runway, knew he was through for the day unless we batted around. Finally, when Lopat was so excited we were afraid he'd explode, Chuck Essegian looked over at him and yelled, "Hey, Eddie, Turk just finished pinch-hitting. He can't go up again."

I played fairly regularly in the outfield the last month of the season. We ended it with an afternoon game against Cleveland. It was a murky, hazy day and Mudcat Grant, one of the fastest and wildest pitchers in the league, was pitching for the Indians. The game meant something to them because they had a shot at fifth place, but it was meaningless to us. We were anchored in eighth.

Lopat, deciding to give the regulars a break started a makeshift lineup, and the Indians just kicked our brains out. With our pitcher scheduled up in the eighth, Eddie looked up and down the bench for a pinch-hitter. Jerry Lumpe, Norm Siebern, and I were sitting together, trying to make ourselves as small as possible because we wanted no part of Mudcat on a day like that.

When Eddie spotted us, he said, "Lumpe, get a bat."

"Not me," Jerry said. "I ain't getting a bat. Mudcat's throwing a little too hard for me today."

"Siebern, you get up there and hit," Lopat said.

"No, thanks," Norm said. "There's about fifteen minutes left to this season and I want to come out of it alive."

Eddie turned to me and said, "All right, Hawk, *you* get a bat."

"Ed, you got the wrong boy," I said. "All I can see is Mudcat's teeth, and I ain't about to walk up to that plate."

The plate umpire was yelling for a hitter, and Lopat was going crazy looking for one. He finally went back to Lumpe and said, "Jerry, *please* hit, will you?"

"Well," Lumpe said, "I'll go up there but I won't guarantee to hit."

He got a bat, went to the plate, took three strikes and came back.

I certainly wanted to make it big in the major leagues, but I didn't intend to be just a journeyman ballplayer, especially when my golf game was so sharp. I was in the low 70s and high 60s regularly, both in and out of the baseball season. I played almost every day, sometimes even going nine holes before afternoon ball games and nine more when they were over.

All the athletes around Kansas City practically lived at Jack Haley's Apartment Lounge. Every year Haley staged a tournament at the Brook Ridge Country Club that had to be the craziest golf event of the year. The Apartment Lounge tournament started like any other, but finished in a shambles, because bikini-clad girls rode around the course in carts with cold beer on ice. Everywhere you turned there was one of those girls handing out a can of Budweiser, and on a hot day you had to be Superman to turn it down.

Well, this particular year the tournament was on an off day for the Athletics, and of course I was among those present. I played in a foursome with Jim Colbert and Rodney Horn, a couple of pros, and a guy from Dallas named Kenny Edwards, whose brother Jerry played on the pro circuit. We nearly always played together anyhow.

Horn was superhuman—he didn't drink and resisted the beer all the way around the course. The rest of us found it necessary to cool our steaming whistles whenever one of those girls came along, and by the time we got through I was a walking Budweiser can.

As we left the eighteenth green, a guy we knew came over and said, "Hawk, I'll bet you Horn can hit the ball farther than you can."

"I know he can't," I said. "I play with him all the time and he hasn't outdriven me yet."

"A hundred bucks says he can right now," the guy said.

Horn was cold sober and I was full of beer, but I took the bet and we went over to the first tee, a three-hundred-yard par 4. Horn drove first and knocked the ball right on the green on his third try. Then he stepped back and said, "That's as far as I can hit it, so there's no sense in my trying any more. If you beat that one, you win."

I had driven that green maybe forty times. But now, bleary-eyed, full of beer, sweating in the afternoon heat, I nearly fell over teeing my ball up. I fanned on my first try, then hit fifteen or sixteen in a row onto a road out of bounds on the left. After that I popped five shots practically straight up in the air. We had agreed to keep hitting until we got one good shot off, but I wasn't going to stay there all day. So sick and tired of swinging I could hardly stand up, I tossed a bill at the guy and said, "Here, take the damn hundred."

Later, while we were sitting around an Olympic-size pool, there was a guy with us who always bragged about the things he could do. He couldn't break 80 but he claimed he had a 2 handicap in golf. He said he was a hell of a softball player, but he couldn't hit the ball as far as second base. He kept talking about what a great card player he was, but he never won. After a while none of us believed anything he said.

While we were sitting there, a fellow named Ray Ewing came along and said to this guy, "How well do you swim?"

"I can swim the length of this pool twice under water without coming up," the guy said.

"I'll bet you can't," Ewing said.

"How much?"

"A hundred."

Now this guy had just finished eighteen holes of golf, had been working on these beers as fast as the rest of us, was smashed and dead tired, and in all the time I had known him had never been able to do any of the things he claimed he could. Figuring this was the easiest way in the world for me to get back the dough I had just lost, I said, "And I'll bet you another hundred."

He took the bets, went in and changed into swimming trunks, then teetered at the edge of the swimming pool, looking as if he was going to fall in. Suddenly he straightened up, went off in a beautiful dive, swam the whole length in about four strokes, turned and zipped right back without once coming up for air, and climbed out.

It sure wasn't my day. It wasn't until later that I learned he had once missed making the U.S. Olympic swimming team by a whisker.

After I left the Athletics, Jack Haley rarely missed a game I played in at Kansas City. He used to rent a bus and take a load of people from the Apartment Lounge to the ball game in it. They'd get tickets on the second deck, right over first base, hang out banners for the Hawk, and cheer every move I made. There were always a couple of those big guys from the football Chiefs, like Curt Merz and Bobby Hunt, to keep anyone from booing me. The minute somebody did, they would get up and the booer would start cheering. I still have the best claque in the league in Kansas City.

Haley, a big guy in his late thirties, had a bit part in the movie *In Cold Blood*. When the movie came to Kansas City, Jack rented half the balcony, had a big party at the Apartment Lounge, and took people to the theater in limousines. They had to be there on time because the only place Jack appears is in the very beginning. A bunch of guys gets off a bus and he's one of them.

His part lasted a second, but you'd think he was the star. He made everybody dress formally, and when they all sat down he kept saying, "Hold it—watch—don't miss it—" before the show even began. When the theater went dark he yelled, "All right— now watch—watch—watch—"

He was still yelling when the movie started. If you kept your eyes glued to the screen, you could see him, but you'd miss him if you looked away for that second. As he stepped off the bus in the picture, we all yelled and the people closest to him shook hands with him and whacked him on the back. Clark Gable couldn't have got a better reception when *Gone with the Wind* opened in Atlanta.

Of course, I still go to the Apartment Lounge now that Kansas City is back in the American League. I not only love it there but it bolsters my ego. Hanging in prominent places are three huge oil paintings. One is of Lenny Dawson, the Chiefs' quarterback. Another is of Lew Krausse pitching.

But the most impressive one of all is of me hitting. I can look at it for hours. Sometimes I do.

9 | Caracas Capers

I am not a troublemaker—just a guy who likes to enjoy life in general and a few laughs in particular, especially after dark. When the Athletics let me go to Caracas to play winter ball after the 1964 season, they forgot to tell the Venezuelans how much I loved fun and games. Caracas is a live town. It doesn't take much looking around to find all the action you can handle.

You don't even have to look around. All you have to do is just be there. There's always something doing and never much to keep you from doing it. Of course, you do have to play baseball, but that's no chore, especially when you break the league record in home runs and runs batted in, as I did. They love baseball in Venezuela, and, if you're a baseball hero down there, the action comes to you.

We had a great gang of guys from the States that year—Bill Bryan, Tommy Helms, Pete Rose, Carl Greene, Duke Sims, Gary Kolb, among others—and there was always something doing. The only disadvantage was homesickness, which begins to set in after you've been around there about a month and gets worse as you go along. Before you're through, everyone is on everyone else's nerves and down everyone else's throats, and even booze doesn't help. You can't wait to get the hell out of there.

One of the most priceless ingredients in Caracas is an apartment. If you're as lucky as I was, you'll find one with a kitchenette where the price is right, the location convenient, and the landlord reasonable. Once you get an apartment, you do anything you can to keep it because the hotel's no bargain, and eating every meal out is a real drag. I like Latin-American food as much as the next guy, but three meals a day of it for three and a half months will make any red-blooded American boy climb the walls.

I shared my apartment with Bill Bryan and Carl Greene, two huge, easygoing guys it was a pleasure to live with under normal circumstances. Bryan was six-four and 225 pounds, Greene six-three and maybe 235. The thing was, although circumstances were perfectly normal starting out, they became less and less so as time went on. By the last month of the winter season, little annoyances were magnified into big problems.

We had a really nice apartment and a good arrangement. Since I couldn't cook worth a lick, Carl and Bill did the cooking and I took care of the dishes. Things worked out fine for the first couple of months, then I began getting edgy. I wanted to see Betty Ann and our little girl, Patricia, in the worst way, and was mad at the Caracas club for not letting me go home, because I was doing so well.

Bill Bryan was just as edgy. He had a girl back home whom he missed something terrible, but she didn't seem to be missing him half as much. He was in a stew over that, I was bitching about not seeing my family, and the only reasonably calm guy in the joint was Carl.

I was pretty good about the dishes until one week I said, "The hell with it," and let them sit in the sink. Nobody said anything while the dirty dishes kept piling up until the sink and the counters were loaded with them and you needed a seeing-eye dog to find a clean coffee cup. The other two guys kept us going by washing just enough dishes for each meal. I refused to so much as turn the water on in the sink.

I got away with it for a few days. After dinner the other two guys used to sit there, waiting for me to get up and do the dishes. I wouldn't move and they wouldn't move for about ten minutes, then one of them would get up and we'd all act is if nothing had happened. We'd sit around for a while and then go to the ball park and play a game before taking in one of the local saloons.

About the fourth day after I went on strike, Bill got a "Dear John" letter from his girl. He was like a bear all day, prowling around the apartment, cursing and yelling at Carl and me, and generally acting like a bastard. Since it happened to be an off night, we took our time eating dinner. Bill and I were grumpy as hell while Carl, a sweet guy who never blew his stack, tried to make conversation.

After we finished eating, we sat at the table for the usual ten minutes without a word. Then Bill said, "Hawk, get your damn ass up and get them dishes washed."

"Man, don't bother me," I growled. "Take them dishes and shove them."

Bill glared at me, and said, "I'm telling you right now, I'm getting sick and tired messing around you, boy. I'm doing all the cooking and washing the dishes, too. My girl's gone and left me, and I'm going to beat your ass if you don't get them dishes washed in a hurry."

"Bill," I said, *"I ain't washing the dishes."*

The two of us stood up, and I knew what was going to happen. That big gorilla was mad enough to kill me and I was fed up enough to try and stop him. When Carl saw us get up, he said, "Listen, we've got the best little deal in Caracas. If you guys fight, we're going to get thrown out sure as hell. Don't do anything. You'll mess the joint up and make enough noise to bring the landlord up here. He'll dump us so fast we won't know what happened."

125

HAWK

I took off my watch and laid it on the table, and Bill hit me with the flat of his hand. I ducked and the blow landed on my shoulder, then I swung and popped him squarely on the mouth. He came back with a belt on my mouth, and the two of us really went at it. As soon as the fight started, Carl said, "Oh, the hell with it," and got his suitcase down off a shelf and began packing it.

The fight was a beauty. I got Bill in the mouth again, then he hit me squarely on the nose—God knows what kept it from breaking —and we whaled away at each other. We weren't just playing. These were fierce punches, and, with neither of us trying to defend himself, every punch was landed on something.

Carl was busy packing when we started on the furniture. The first thing we got was the kitchen table. We crashed into it and the thing crumpled like a piece of cardboard. We kept on swinging away, sometimes hitting each other, sometimes hitting whatever happened to be in the way.

The next thing to go was a really nice chair in the living room— one of those rattan things with soft deep cushions. While the cushions went flying, the chair fell apart just way the way the table had. There was blood all over the place—on the walls, on the rugs, even on the ceiling—and still we went at it.

A full-length mirror leaning against the wall didn't have a chance. When we crashed into that, it broke in a million pieces, carving us up a little, but we had cut each other so badly we didn't even notice it. Sooner or later, we both got pooped, and started wrestling around. We landed on another nice chair, smashing that to pieces, and then broke an end table and a big lamp that was on it.

By this time, we could hardly lift our arms, we were so tired. We were swinging like a couple of zombies, not hurting each other any more, just belting away. The whole damn apartment was a shambles, and neither Bill nor I could move. We finally ran out of gas so completely that we couldn't stand up.

The place was a terrible mess. Bill and I looked at each other, then looked around and one of us said, "For crissakes, did we do all this?"

"You're damn right you did," Carl said. "I'm packed and ready to go. You guys better do the same thing because that landlord's going to be here any minute."

Bill and I got our suitcases down and were packing when there was a knock on the door. It was the landlord yelling in Spanish, "What's going on here?"

Carl let him in, and when he saw the job we had done, he rolled his eyes, shook his fists, waved his arms, and was jabbering so fast we couldn't understand him. He didn't have to look very far to see who had been fighting. Carl was neat and clean, while Bill and I were a mass of bruises. The two of us were still bleeding from cuts and punches, and we were both trying to pack without getting our stuff all stained with blood.

The landlord finally slowed down to a speaking pace we could understand and said, "If you're not out of here by nine o'clock in the morning, I'll get the police. You hear me? Nine o'clock! Not one minute later. I'm coming down to check, and you better not be here."

When he stormed out, the three of us sat on the beds—the only furniture we hadn't ruined—and rolled around laughing. We sure had loused up our wonderful deal, but it was worth it.

"A hell of a fight," Carl said. "So help me, the best I ever saw. I wish I had a movie camera. That thing should have been recorded for posterity. Guys would pay a hundred bucks to see it."

After we were packed, Bill said, "Let's go go-cart racing."

"Hell of an idea," I said.

Bill and I washed some of the blood off ourselves, I put my watch back on my wrist, and the three of us started out. Carl was the only one who looked civilized. Bill had a black eye and I had a lip puffed out so far I could see it without looking in a mirror. The two of us had cuts all over our faces, and we still were dabbing blood off with handkerchiefs as we left the building.

We ran into a couple of other ballplayers at the go-cart races— Gary Kolb, Jim McKnight, maybe a half dozen guys altogether— and we closed the joint up. Then we stopped in for a few beers, went back to the apartment, and fell into bed.

The next morning we were out by nine o'clock and checked into the hotel where most of the others were staying. The three of us took a room together, and that was where we lived in peace and quiet until it was time to go home. We ate all our meals out. Although we got kind of sick of it, we only had to hang around a couple more weeks, so it wasn't too bad. At least we didn't have any more dishwashing problems.

I sure didn't have any problems on the field. I hit the hell out of the ball all season. El Hawko was the big slugger of the league, once hitting three homers in one game. I don't think anyone ever did that in the Venezuelan League before or since. But as my home-sickness increased and my disposition soured, lousy umpires' decisions, bad breaks, and fielders robbing me of extra-base hits made me madder and madder.

One night I was thrown out of a game for banging my batting helmet on the ground after a called third strike which must have been a foot wide of the plate. But that was nothing compared to the battle I had during an interleague game with a club from the Dominican Republic.

The game was close and the umpires had been doing things wrong all night. When one of them, a guy named Armando Rodriguez, called one of those ridiculous third strikes on me with two out and a couple of men on bases, I blew my cork. While I screamed in English and he screamed back in Spanish, we got closer and closer to each other.

Finally, we got too close and I couldn't resist the temptation to belt him. Down he went, and, man, was I in the soup! The one thing no professional ballplayer can get away with anywhere is to sock an umpire. It calls for just as stiff a penalty in Latin-American countries as it does here, and I knew it. The other umpires came over, along with our manager, Reggie Otero, and I got the bum's rush faster than you can say Hawk.

I drew a fifteen-day suspension and a fine of two thousand bolivars. I didn't mind the suspension—that carried me almost to the end of the season, but when my translation of two thousand bolivars came to four hundred and forty-five dollars in American money, I raised a terrible stink. Since I had ten or twelve homers leading the league and was one of its best drawing cards, even the owners of the other clubs didn't want me out for fifteen days. They all got together and made a special ruling, cutting the suspension down to five days and the fine in half. To hit the umpire was worth one thousand bolivars to me, but not two.

The night Duke Sims and I broke the table arm-wrestling was one of the daffiest of the season down there. After the game we had a few drinks, then ate a huge meal, spiced with all kinds of junk, and garnished with several beers. By then it was after midnight, and Tommy Helms, sitting next to me at dinner, said, "How fast can you run, Hawk?"

"I can outrun your ass," I said.

"The hell you can," he said. "I'll give you five yards and beat you in sixty for a hundred bucks."

"O.K.," I said. "Where do we race?"

"Right out on the street," Tommy said.

Caracas is a big town, the restaurant was on the main drag, and, although traffic wasn't as heavy as in the daytime, there were plenty of cars still out.

"Man," I said, "you're crazy as hell. You think all those cars are going to stop for us to have a race?"

"We'll stop 'em," Helms said.

The whole gang of us went out to the front of the restaurant. While Bill Bryan and Pete Rose stood with their hands up to stop traffic, a couple of other guys paced off sixty yards. By then, horns were honking and drivers were yelling, and pretty soon a cop came over. When Bill told him we were going to have a race, he grinned, then told the nearest drivers, who passed the word back. People were out of cars and pedestrians were lining the sidewalk by the time we got started.

Somebody paced off my five yards, and I beat Tommy so badly I wouldn't have needed the handicap. The people were cheering and yelling and clapping. When I got back to the starting line Rose said, "I'll race you for a hundred, too."

"How much will you give me?" I said.

"Seven yards."

Most of the people knew who we were, and while my new handicap was being paced off, I heard one guy yell "Hawk," and another yell "Pete," and they put fingers up. Pretty soon everybody was yelling names and putting fingers up. The whole street was full of guys placing bets.

That Rose can fly. He passed me before I had taken five steps, and beat me by ten yards. When we got back to where we started, Helms said, "Give me seven yards, Pete, and I'll beat you for a hundred."

By the time Tommy was at his seven-yard mark, the street was alive with bets again. A couple more cops came to help hold up the traffic, but nobody was moving anyhow. Everyone was too busy placing bets on Helms and Rose. I thought Rose would murder him the way he murdered me, but Helms held on to the finish and beat him by a stride.

Now we were all even. Tommy paid me my hundred, I gave it to Pete and he handed it back to Tommy. I looked around and saw people paying each other all over the street. But as I looked, the lights started running together and I thought of those arm-wrestling matches with Duke and the ball game and the drinks and the spicy meal and the beer and the races, and I smelled the gas fumes from all the cars starting up, and I knew I wasn't going to hold a thing. I staggered to the gutter and everything came up. Just as I finished, I heard Helms burp, and off he went. That Rose must have a cast-iron stomach. He and Bryan just stood there and laughed.

One night I went to a men's bar and restaurant with Bryan and Greene for dinner. We were the only Americans in the place, but the guys at the next table spoke English. As soon as they saw us, they began ripping hell out of the United States, calling us Communists, of all things. We took it for a while, but when one guy turned and yelled, "You're worse than Communists—you're damned American bastards," I had had it.

I stood up and said, "If I were you, I'd keep quiet. You've been drinking too much and you don't what you're saying, so just shut up."

He came at me with a bottle, and I belted him. As he got up, he pulled out a knife, and when he started for me, Bryan picked up a chair, hit him over the head with it, knocked him cold, and said, "Come on, let's get the hell out of here."

We went for the door, tossed some dough for our meal at the cashier, and made it to a taxi. I don't know what kind of a mess we left behind, but we could see that the place was full of guys yelling and fighting as the cab pulled away from there.

I had a lot of good Venezuelan friends down there who made a bullfight *aficionado* out of me. They knew I was an all-round athlete after the *Universal,* one of the Caracas newspapers, had run a picture of me holding a baseball, a golf club, a football, and a basketball. One day a guy said, "Hawk, did you ever try bull-fighting?"

"I've never tried it," I said, "but it sure doesn't look tough. All you have to do is let the bull come at you and knife him in the right place as he goes by."

"It isn't exactly that easy," the guy said. "We have baby bulls of our own we fool around with on Sundays when there aren't any fights in town. How about coming out with us next week?"

It sounded great to me. The group was made up of rich young guys who liked to take their girls out to watch them practice on these baby bulls. Just to make sure nobody got hurt, they put plastic caps on the bulls' horns and used blunted sticks to protect the animals. They'd make passes just like in the regular ring, and at the end judges would decide whether the guy or the bull won.

They picked me up the following Sunday and drove me maybe thirty miles out of town to somebody's ranch, where they had a bull ring set up. Everybody was dressed casually—none of those fancy costumes real bullfighters wear—and everything was very informal. They told me dungarees and a T shirt and tennis shoes would be fine. Most were dressed the same, although a few wore Bermuda shorts.

There were maybe a hundred people sitting in a makeshift grandstand, and the more I watched, the more convinced I was I could become the greatest bullfighter in baseball history. As I sat there, maybe half a dozen mock fights were held. The baby bulls, their horns covered, would be let loose out of a corral on the other side of the ring, and the "fighter" would flare out his cape and tease the bulls while everyone yelled *"Olé"* and all that. When it was over, a few guys would herd the bull back to the corral and wait for the next event.

Finally somebody said, "What do you think, Hawk? Do you want to try it?"

"Sure," I said, and I jumped down to the ring. Somebody tossed me a cape, and I posed at one end waiting for the baby bull to come out of the other.

132

I stood there making practice passes and pirouetting around and listening to all the *"Olés"* when they opened the gate at the opposite side of the ring to let the bull out. Instead of a baby with caps on his horns, out came a full-sized bull with no caps, snorting and fussing and kicking up dust as he charged at me. I took one look at the big bare horns on that sonofagun, dropped the cape, and ran. You never saw a guy jump a fence faster than I did, and everyone was laughing like hell as I tumbled into the stands.

It took me only a minute to understand that I had been had. This was standard procedure, an initiation for newcomers to the gentle art of bullfighting. It happened to every stranger who thought it looked easy and wanted to try his luck without risking his neck. I was still shaking when one of the guys came over and said, "You did fine, Hawk. Now if you want to go out there again, we'll really use a baby bull with his horns capped. What do you say?"

"No, thanks," I said. "I've had enough of this. Just take me to the nearest golf course and drop me off."

That was the last time I ever stuck my nose up at bullfighters.

Near the end of the season we gave Jim McKnight a farewell party at a big bar in town. I guess every American ballplayer in Caracas was at the affair because Jim was a hell of a guy and everybody liked him. We had the usual—a few drinks, a big meal, some beer—the whole bit.

Late in the evening Tommy Helms, who's a little guy—he stands only five-ten—got into an argument with a huge Venezuelan. I don't know who started it, how, or why, but the Venezuelan suddenly drilled Tommy so hard he knocked him all the way across the floor out cold. As he went for Tommy, I went for him and got there just in time to keep him from kicking Tommy while he was on the floor. The guy turned and swung on me, one of our gang started to my rescue, a Venezuelan started to his, and the next thing you knew, there was one of the greatest Donnybrooks I've ever seen.

It seemed as if there wasn't a man in the house not fighting with somebody. Every one of us was swinging blindly on whoever happened to be around, and if the fight had lasted, we would all have been creamed because we were outnumbered by about ten to one. I had long since forgotten the guy who hit Tommy and was still swinging my arms at the nearest target when a guy suddenly came up to me and stuck a gun in my stomach.

I said, "Oh, God, what a way to go," and stood petrified before one single Spanish word came to me. All I could think of was "time out," so I said, *"Tiempo—tiempo—tiempo—"*

He jerked his head toward the door and said, *"Policia,"* and I thought, "Well, jeez, the guy isn't going to shoot me." When we got outside, I tried to explain that I hadn't started it, but he couldn't speak any English and what little Spanish I had was lost in that fight.

Then I said, "I'm a ballplayer—ballplayer—"

He nodded, but kept the gun on me while he hailed a taxi and hauled me off to the pokey. The crowning insult came when he made me pay the fare. When we got inside I figured somebody would give me a break because I was a ballplayer. The desk where the sergeant sat was so high it came up to my shoulders. I reached up with one hand, smiled at the guy and said, "Baseball player—El Hawko," but he slapped my hand off the desk and I knew I wasn't going to get any help there.

Finally I said in English, "I want to call the American Consulate."

The sergeant shook his head, said something to the guy who had pinched me, and they emptied my pockets and put me in a little cell next to one that must have had forty people in it—men and women screaming and cursing and fighting and pushing each other around. But the worst thing about it was the smell. The whole joint stank of every nauseating odor imaginable, and a few that were new to me.

Ten minutes after I was locked up, they brought in the big guy who had started the whole thing—the one who had flattened Helms. The two of us looked at each other, grinned, and shook hands. He knew a little English, and turned out to be a pretty nice guy. The two of us sat on a bench and were talking when Manager Reggie Otero of the Caracas ball club came along. I never was so happy to see anyone in my life.

"Get me out of here, Reggie," I said.

"I can't," he said. "They've got a rule that if you get put in jail after one in the morning you have to spend the night there."

"Well, jeez, Reggie," I said, "I don't know why they picked on me. I didn't start the damn fight. Even the owner of the joint knows that."

"I'm sorry, Hawk," Otero said, "but I can't do a thing. I'll get you out first thing in the morning."

I spent most of the night yakking with my roommate and trying to ignore the horrible stink from next door. To make things worse, it started raining, and the roof leaked. I might have got an hour's sleep, but no more, and I was a pretty sorry mess when they finally came around at six in the morning to spring me.

Somehow or other, I managed to stay out of trouble for the rest of the season. Happy as I was to go home, I must admit it was fun while it lasted. Someday, when I get too old to fight, maybe I'll go back and look up old friends.

And if they'll guarantee to stick to babies, I may even try bullfighting again.

10 | Life with Finley

Charley Finley wasn't the smartest baseball owner I ever knew, but he sure as hell was the most interesting. With him in charge, you never had to worry about being bored to death. Whether or not it made sense, he was always doing something. If he wasn't firing a manager, he was hiring a pinch-runner, or moving a franchise, or dreaming up a gag, or shaking up the front office.

There were times when he was like a father to me and times when he made life miserable for me. In general, we got along pretty well, probably because we were both off-beat guys who recognized and sort of admired each other as such. But we were like a married couple with problems—buddy-buddy one minute and deadly enemies the next. Up to 1969, Charley hadn't spoken to me in two years. That wasn't my fault. Every time I approached him, whenever we happened to be in the same place, he turned around and walked the other way.

I never could understand why he stayed mad at me. I didn't walk out on him; he fired me. He lent me a lot of dough, but I paid every cent of it back. I went along with his gags, obeyed most of his orders even when they made no sense, was always loyal to him and his ball club, gave everything I had, and hit well in a park that was murder for right-handed sluggers like me.

137

Naturally, we had our little differences, but they really weren't too serious. You couldn't work for Charley Finley, either on or off the field, without having differences. He was turbulent, stubborn, opinionated, and at times impossible. Yet he could be the sweetest guy in the world. I valued his friendship when I had it and would welcome it any time he wants to extend it to me again.

Most of our troubles were financial. You see, Charley lent me plenty. At one time I owed him more than the salary he was paying me. I've always been a big spender. I like nice things and nice things cost money. There are only so many ways you can make it, and if my luck was lousy, I was always running out of ways. Charley used to give me hell for my extravagances, and of course he was right. But since I couldn't stop spending, the only way I could get out from under my load of debts—Finley wasn't my only creditor—was by hitting the jackpot somewhere along the line.

While I could always make an honest dollar on the golf course or at the pool table, my real hope was to bat my way out of debt. When I first went up to the Athletics I was making the major-league minimum salary, which was seventy-five hundred a year. I didn't get any raises the first two years because I was up and down between the majors and the minors. I started the 1963 season in Portland and ended it in Kansas City, then started the 1964 season in Kansas City and ended it in Dallas in the Pacific Coast League.

As anyone can plainly see, this is not the way to make big money out of professional baseball. Finley gave me a break when the 1965 season began—a big, fat five-hundred-dollar raise to eight thousand. With Mel McGaha managing, I had a hell of a year, hitting twenty-three home runs and staying with the Athletics all season. It was, incidentally, my only full season with them.

Although I figured a thousand bucks a home run was not unreasonable, I was very decent with Charley about my 1966 contract. All I asked was double my 1965 salary—sixteen thousand. I thought that was more than fair. Charley disagreed. We settled for twelve thousand dollars—a pittance. Hell, between Charley and a few others, I owed more than that.

Still, sooner or later it was obvious that Charley would have to pay me the kind of dough I could live on, have all these nice things I needed, and get my debts paid off. But when he was paying me while I was owing him, you can see that the situation was sort of hairy. Charley could have solved it easily. All he had to do to wipe me off his books was give me a raise covering my debt to him, but we never really got together on that point.

The first time Charley lent me money was the year I went up to the Athletics from Portland. I went broke paying my own expenses in Kansas City while keeping Betty Ann and the baby in Portland. We didn't dare give up the house there because I never knew when Finley might just get it into his head to send me back. When I went to him for help he lent me a thousand dollars, which took some of the pressure off.

When we finally went to Kansas City to stay, we decided to buy a house, but I didn't have a dime. I was hitting the hell out of the ball for eight thousand dollars a year. I'd like to have asked for a bonus or a new contract, but knew I couldn't get one. So I just went to Finley and said, "Charley, I need some money to get a house."

He was real agreeable and friendly. "Don't worry, Kenny," he said. "We'll get you a house and we'll get you some furniture to put into it. Only are you sure you want to buy here in Kansas City?"

I had been hearing rumors about the Athletics' moving out of there—they finally went to Oakland in 1968—ever since I joined the organization. But I had a love affair going with Kansas City. I liked the town and the people there liked me, and I thought it would be great to live there.

"I'm sure," I said.

He lent me five or six thousand for a down payment on the house and furniture, and we moved right in. I couldn't have done it if Charley hadn't helped me, and I really appreciated it. On the other hand, we agreed that he'd take regular payments out of my salary, and pretty soon I was back up to my ears in debt. I couldn't live on eight thousand dollars, let alone any less. I had to scratch around, picking up dough wherever I could, but I was running a losing race with my creditors, who were piling up like flies.

In the meantime, I continued to have a hell of a year. The fans loved me—used to yell "Hawk—Hawk—Hawk—" every time I did something, and gave me standing ovations when I hit a home run or made a good fielding play. And life with Finley wasn't too bad. I was his favorite ballplayer, although there were times when I know I aggravated the hell out of him.

He didn't mind my talking back and forth with the fans—I always had something going with somebody up in the stands—but he went crazy when I threw baseballs to them. When I played the outfield and caught a ball close to the stands or picked up a long foul that came out there, I sometimes turned and threw it to the customers. They loved it and I loved it and everyone had a good time except Charley.

He'd sit in his box and burn, and after the game send for me and really eat me out.

"Dammit, Kenny," he'd say, "those balls cost money. I don't mind when someone hits one in, but there's no reason for you to throw them in deliberately. That's just plain waste."

And I'd say, "But Charley, it's great for the club. You couldn't buy that kind of good will for the price of a ball."

And he'd say, "If everyone on the club felt that way, you guys would break me in a season."

He raised hell about three-seventy-five baseballs while spending thousands on uniforms we hated. The green ones and the white ones were O.K., but the gold ones were awful. We had to wear them both at home and on the road because Finley made us open every series with them. If we had three games with the same club at home, for example, we'd wear the gold ones the first day and the white ones the next two. We'd also have to open the road series with the gold uniforms, and then switch to green.

We squawked regularly about it, especially to Alvin Dark when he became the manager in 1966. Dark didn't like the gold uniforms any better than we did.

"Look," Alvin would tell Charley, "my boys are playing good ball. They hate those gold uniforms. Why do you make them wear them?"

"It's my ball club," Charley would say, "and they'll wear what I want them to."

I beefed as much as everyone else about the gold uniforms, but they didn't bother me as much as Charley's insistence that we wear our socks real low. I always wore mine high—still do—because I think those pants all the way down to your ankles look like hell. Charley sent memos down to the locker room ordering us to wear our socks low and I'd ignore them. Then he'd call me up to the office and give me hell.

"What do you think I send those memos down for—my health?" he'd shout. "You wear your socks low like everyone else."

"What the hell difference does it make?" I'd say. "Those low socks make your pants look baggy. I have to wear my pants high and tight to be comfortable. I don't want to go out looking like a 1910 ballplayer."

Catfish Hunter felt the same way I did, but he didn't squawk so much. I guess he didn't get to see Charley that often. He wore high socks when he knew Charley wouldn't be at the ball game, but mine were always high.

Dark, who didn't give a damn how I wore my socks, warned me Finley was getting madder and madder at me.

"He's after me about you all the time, Hawk," Alvin used to say. "He'll fine you sure."

"Look," I'd say, "one thing he won't do is fine me. What the hell, he's taking enough out of my salary as it is."

One day Charley was in New York when we played a doubleheader with the Yankees. In the first game I wore my socks high, as usual, and had a hell of a game—two or three hits, a home run— and we won it. Between games Al Zych, the equipment manager, came over and said, "Hawk, you'd better get those socks off. Charley's going to fine you a hundred bucks if you don't."

"You've got to be kidding," I said. "After the game I had—"

"Well, he sent word down."

"O.K.," I said. "You give me the lowest pair of socks you've got. And a pair of 38 pants (I wear size 31), a 48 shirt (I wear 42), and a 7½ cap (I wear 7¼). And when I go out there, I hope the sonofagun is happy."

Al got all this stuff, and I wore the socks so low you couldn't see anything but the white undersocks. My pants were baggy, my shirt looked like a balloon, and my cap was down over my ears. When I showed up on the field, everybody roared. I looked over at Charley beside our dugout, and he was fuming. But he couldn't say a word. And he never again bugged me about my high socks.

Charley's great pride and joy was his mule, Charley O. The mule grazed at the ball park in Kansas City and was almost always in sight of the crowd there. Charley O. was really a great gimmick, and the fans got as big a kick out of him as Finley did. As a matter of fact, I always thought the mule looked like Charley.

Charley O. was pretty much of a homebody. So far as I knew, he never traveled—just was kept around the ball park for when the team was home. But one year—either 1966 or 1967, because it was when Dark managed the club—Finley announced that the mule would take some selected trips so that fans in other American League parks could see him. Nobody took him seriously. It didn't seem possible that Finley would pay all those shipping charges just for a gag.

One day in New York, just before a game at Yankee Stadium, Charley came into the clubhouse and said, "Anybody know how to ride a mule?"

"I can," I said.

I didn't know whether I could or not. The only time I'd ever been on a mule was at my grandma's farm in Woodruff when I was a kid. They had a little saddle for me and my grandma or grandpa would lead the mule around in case he started bucking. But I figured there must be some money or a gift or something in here somewhere. If I rode the mule for Charley, he'd give me a nice present or maybe not take anything out of my next pay check.

"O.K., Kenny," Charley said, "I want you to ride this mule around the ball park before the game."

I thought the mule would be saddled, but all he had was a blanket on his back. Well, I put the beak of my cap up like a jockey, and, while a couple of guys held Charley O., somebody helped me get aboard him. I thought it might be like riding a horse, but it wasn't. A horse has a little flexibility, and if he's handled right runs pretty smoothly. But a mule has big, bumpy shoulders and runs so wobbly you bounce all over the place and have to hang on like mad to keep from being thrown.

We started out on the track in right field, and I got the mule trotting pretty well as we followed the foul line toward the plate. We were maybe halfway down, approaching the Yankee dugout, when Charley O. began cantering, and I lost control of him. I got scared, the mule sensed it, and the next thing I knew, he was madly dashing along while I frantically hung on to whatever part of his anatomy I could get a grip on.

I tried to wrap my arms around his neck, but he was bucking so hard that I couldn't get a real hold on him. Suddenly, he bounced me almost off and I just reached out with arms and legs. Somehow,

I ended up with all four of my limbs around his neck, but riding upside down. By then we were right in front of the Yankee dugout. I saw just enough to realize that everyone in it was holding his sides laughing, and a few guys were hanging on to each other to keep from falling.

I knew the whole stadium was rocking with laughter, but I was too busy to look. All I wanted now was to get off the damn animal. Bill Jones, our trainer, was chasing us, figuring I'd break a few bones, at least, when I fell, as I surely would. Somebody hit Charley O. with a baseball, I guess—at least it sounded like a baseball—then, as we passed the Athletics dugout, Orlando Pena slapped him on the fanny with a fungo bat.

Charley O. kept on going, now heading along the foul line toward left field. But he was beginning to slow up, I think because I was cutting off his wind with those death-tight grips of my arms and legs on his neck. He finally got down to a pace where I could slide off without getting killed. I skidded along the ground a little way, and then stopped and struggled to my feet while the crowd roared.

I ran in, bowing in all directions and waving my cap. When I approached the dugout, I saw Charley Finley in the box beside it wiping his eyes with one hand and slapping his knee with the other, absolutely and completely broken up. Practically everyone in our dugout was roaring, too, everyone but Alvin, that is.

"My heavens, that was the dumbest thing I ever saw," he said. "You could have been killed. If that man wants a jockey, he ought to go out and hire one. I don't ever want him risking one of my ballplayers on that mule again."

I guess he and Finley had it out later—they were always having something out—but Charley didn't give a damn. He got what he wanted—a hell of a good laugh and plenty of ink in that lush New York market. The papers had big stories about Charley O. and me, and I guess they all carried pictures of me on and under him. I had hoped Finley might shell out a little dough, but, since I then had a big thing for headgear, crazy and otherwise, he gave me a twenty-five-dollar Stetson instead.

Either that day or the next, Finley announced he was shipping Charley O. to Chicago when we played there to give the Comiskey Park fans a chance to see him. At the time, he and Arthur Allyn, the White Sox owner, were feuding—for all I know they may be still—and Allyn promptly announced that neither Finley nor his mule would be allowed in the ball park.

This didn't bother Charley. He rented a band, which he put in a parking lot across the street from the ball park, and had the boys play numbers like "Everything's Up to Date in Kansas City" and "Charley Rode a Mule" and stuff like that. Allyn had cops stationed at every entrance with orders not to let either Finley or Charley O. in.

The ball game started, with no sign of either. I didn't play that day and was in the clubhouse having a smoke when I heard a commotion outside the door, then a knock. When I opened it, there was Charley giving orders in a stage whisper to a crew of guys pulling and pushing a huge box, five or six feet high and so wide it wouldn't fit through the door.

Panting with excitement, grinning foolishly, his eyes as big as saucers, Charley said, "Come on, Kenny, help us get this box open."

"What's in it?" I said.

"Never mind, never mind, just let's get it open quick."

Inside was a mule—not Charley O., he was too big—but a baby mule that looked just like him.

"Come on, come on," Finley whispered. "Let's get him out—hurry up—"

Then, when we had coaxed and hauled and yanked the animal

out of the box, Finley said, "Kenny, help me get this thing on the field."

"You can't take him on the field, Charley," I said. "It's right in the middle of the ball game."

"I don't give a damn when it is," he said. "I got the mule this far and we're going to get him the rest of the way. Now, come on. Are you going to help me or not?"

There was a threat in just the way he said it. I'm a game guy, but I know when I'm licked. This man was my boss. He was giving me orders to help him push a baby mule through the runway to the dugout and the ball field. Who was I to argue with him?

The mule wasn't too cooperative, and we had quite a time just getting him down the steps. The runway at Comiskey Park is narrow and sometimes slippery, because water leaks down from somewhere and it's often wet. Charley had a rope around the mule's neck, and was hauling him from the front. I was in back pushing, a position I didn't like one damn bit.

I stayed as close to the side as I could, ready to jump any minute the mule might kick, while Charley, still talking in his stage whisper, kept after me to push harder. We finally got the mule to the foot of the dugout steps, while the ballplayers on the bench nearest the runway collapsed. They couldn't believe what they were seeing. I noticed Alvin Dark's eyes go narrow, and I knew he was about to blow his stack. It was a tight game, the White Sox had men on base, and Jack Aker was on the mound, concentrating on the hitter.

"Kenny," Finley whispered, "help me push him up the steps to the field so the customers can see him."

"Charley," I said, "we can't do this."

"The hell we can't."

So we both got in back of the mule and pushed him up the steps. Once on the field, he just started running around and you could hear the ripples of laughter from all over the stands. One of the base umpires was the first to see what was going on, and he called time while Jack was winding up to pitch.

Charley, hee-hawing until tears were streaming down his face, pointed up at Allyn's box while the mule galloped around and the fans went nuts. I just ducked down the dugout steps and cringed. Dark was boiling, the White Sox owner was boiling, and Aker, whose concentration had been shattered, must have been boiling out there on the mound. All I wanted to do was disappear.

The plate umpire—I think it was Frankie Munn—came marching over to our dugout yelling, "Get that damn thing out of here." Then, spotting me, he yelled, "Come on, Hawk. I know you brought him in. Get him out."

I was up to here with mules, and I wasn't about to chase this one down. As it happened, he hadn't gone very far, and a few of the guys managed to get him back to the top of the dugout steps. Then Finley, still laughing like mad, said, "All right, Kenny, let's take him back."

Just as he said it, the mule, backing down the steps at the runway, stepped on my foot, and I howled because it hurt like hell.

"Let somebody else get him back," I said. "He just stepped on my foot."

"Don't worry about it," Finley said.

What the hell, it wasn't his foot.

We got the mule back through the runway, up the clubhouse steps, and back into the box at the door, while Charley babbled away, happy as a kid with a lollipop. He gave me fifty bucks that time, I think, but he shortchanged me. I couldn't play for three days on account of my foot.

Finley once shipped Charley O. all the way to Los Angeles. Charley told me to ride him and, like a dope, I agreed. We started at home plate in Dodger Stadium, where the Angels played their home games that year, then went down the left-field foul line and headed around the track fringing the outfield. Everything was fine

—I was sort of used to Charley O. and had him running about as smoothly as a mule could—and the crowd cheered while I waved my cap.

I was so busy waving that I didn't notice a kid leaning out of the bleachers dangling a hot dog practically in front of Charley O.'s nose. The minute the mule saw it he stopped short, and you know what happened to me. I started right over the top of his head.

I made a frantic grab for his mane to keep from falling, and the next thing I knew we were eyeball to eyeball. I was upside down, looking right into the mule's big soft brown eyes while he calmly stood munching the hot dog the kid had given him.

Finally, I managed to get on his back again. I hit him in the rump and said, "Come on, Charley, let's go," but Charley O. wasn't having any. People were feeding him peanuts and popcorn and hot dogs, and he was having the time of his life. We must have been there ten minutes while I kept yelling up to the fans, "Please stop feeding him. He won't move until you do."

Seems to me I got fifty or a hundred from Finley for that ride. And, if I'm not mistaken, it was my last appearance on Charley O. I know Catfish Hunter wanted to ride him, and Diego Segui, a farm boy from Cuba, rode him a couple of times.

In the meantime, my financial situation got worse. Even with the raise to twelve thousand dollars in 1966, I couldn't keep up with my debts. I got off to a terrible start, but it wasn't all my fault. The Kansas City ball park had a long left-field line, and I often hit outs that would have been homers anywhere else. It was getting me down, and Alvin knew it. He kept saying, "Hawk, don't let this park beat you." But I *was* letting the park beat me—hitting poorly, not fielding well, down in the dumps—and in June the Athletics traded me to Washington.

Much as I disliked leaving Alvin, at least now I figured I'd get my full salary. But Charley Finley had left no stone unturned in

making sure he would continue to collect from me. He simply ar-
ranged for the Senators to take his pound of flesh out of my pay-
check and send it along to him. Although I squawked to General
Manager George Selkirk, they did it for the rest of that season.

However, George finally saw my point. As the 1967 season
began, he told Finley that my financial troubles were so bad he
feared it would affect my play, and he refused to send Finley any
more money. Now, at last, I was a twelve-thousand-dollar ballplayer actually collecting twelve thousand dollars.

11 | Gil Hodges and Me

With Gil Hodges and me, it was a case of dislike at first sight. The personality clash between us was instant. After my first month at Washington, there wasn't a day that I didn't wish I were somewhere else. One of the happiest moments of my life came when the Senators sold me back to Kansas City. That was in June 1967, after I had played part of two seasons under Hodges' management.

Don't get me wrong—the guy was by no means all bad. He transformed me from a second-rate first baseman into a good one, for he knew the position and how to teach it. He worked like hell with me, and I appreciated that. But, in general, he treated his ballplayers like dogs, and I was no exception. I don't know how the Mets, whom he now manages, feel about him, but I can tell you without reservation that every Washington player he ever had hated his guts.

Still, when I think about him, I don't have to grope for one other thing to say in his favor. Away from the baseball atmosphere he was a hell of a guy. He once threw a party for the whole ball club at his bowling alley in Brooklyn, and I've never been entertained by a nicer host. And his son, Gilly, is a real sweetheart, a wonderful kid whom everyone liked.

151

HAWK

Hodges gets a marvelous press—I don't know of any baseball figure with a better public image—but that's because he plays up to the writers and sportscasters. They'll all—especially in New York—tell you there's no nicer guy in baseball. If I saw him only under the conditions they do I'd agree with them.

Having disposed of all the hearts and flowers, now I'll tell you about the Dr. Jekyll and Mr. Hyde that is the Gil Hodges I knew. Maybe he's old Mr. Lovable with the Mets, but at Washington he was unfair, unreasonable, unfeeling, incapable of handling men, stubborn, holier-than-thou, and ice cold. I can't say he played favorites, because he didn't have any favorites. It would be more accurate to say that he played the guys he disliked the least. I don't think he actually liked any of us, and I know none of us liked him. He was impossible to play for because he was impossible to understand.

There were guys on that team with whom he didn't exchange one word during the whole time I was with the Senators. One regular hadn't been on speaking terms with him from the week after his first season as the Washington manager to the day he left to manage the Mets. They didn't even speak at the bowling party.

I once asked the ballplayer, "Why don't you and Hodges ever talk?"

"I'll tell you exactly why," he said. "I had a bad start his first season here. One night, after I had struck out three or four times I said, 'Gil, what do you think I'm doing wrong at the plate?'

" 'How the hell am I supposed to know what you're doing wrong at the plate?' Hodges said. 'You've got to work that out yourself.'

"I got up and walked out and we haven't spoken since."

Hodges ate guys out in front of the whole team for things they had done wrong long before. He acted as if he had something personal against every man on his squad. Joining the Senators was like starting a prison term. Hodges was the warden, expecting the worst from everyone.

He had absolutely no sense of humor. He smiled and kidded with the writers, especially when we were in New York, but he never kidded with us. I don't mind a tough manager—and heaven knows Hodges was tough—as long as he can see at least a glimmer of the funny side of life. Hodges was the only manager I ever had who never saw anything funny in what anybody said or did, never came out with a wisecrack when alone with his ballplayers, never did or said anything to relieve the tensions that plague every ball club.

I didn't know any of these things when I first reported to Hodges. I had never met him, but didn't like what I had heard about him from his own ballplayers. Whenever we played the Senators, we heard weird stories about the horrible relationships between the manager and his men. I don't know how many guys on that club would come up to me and say, "You don't know how lucky you are. Your owner's a screwball, but a funny guy. Your manager's great and an understanding guy. We hardly know our owner, and our manager's a cold-blooded tyrant."

Actually, my first meeting with Hodges was pleasant enough. The instantaneous mutual dislike was there, all right, but it was under the surface. I just had the feeling that he didn't approve of me. And, of course, after all I'd heard about him, I was wary of him and prepared to dislike him.

I reported to his office in the clubhouse at Washington on June 23, 1966. We were playing the Detroit Tigers, with Earl Wilson pitching for them. After Hodges and I shook hands, he said, "I know you're going bad, but I know the type of ballplayer you are and the type of ballplayer you can be."

Then he said, "I know you've got good hands. I know you can play first base better than you've been playing it. I know you can hit better. You're just the way I was at your age. While you're here, we're going to make you a good first baseman or no first baseman at all."

"All right," I said.

"And I don't want you to play any golf," he said.

That was something of a blow. Alvin had let me play because he thought it relaxed me. But when Hodges ordered me to quit, I told him I would, and I did.

At the time, I had been running the bases very well—I guess it was about the only thing I had done right at Kansas City that year. I had stolen nine bases in nine tries and had more steals than anybody on the Washington club. Alvin had let me run on my own.

"Do you let any of the guys run on their own here?" I asked Hodges.

"No," he said. "Nobody but Valentine. I'll give you the signal when I want you to go."

"I was nine for nine over in Kansas City," I said. "I can steal a base for you."

"I'll decide when you'll steal a base."

"I might help the ball club," I said. "I usually can tell when a pitcher will throw a breaking ball or an off-speed pitch, and those are the kinds I can steal on."

Hodges glared at me and said, "I told you I'll give you the sign when I want you to steal."

That was the end of the interview. And all during the time I played for him, Hodges didn't once give me the steal sign.

I walked out that night with ambivalent feelings about the guy. Except for the little unpleasantness about stealing, it had been a nice talk. He obviously felt I was a better ballplayer than I had looked in Kansas City and obviously was prepared to help me. I decided maybe I had made a mistake accepting what others said about Hodges as gospel. I'd go by what I saw myself, not what I had heard.

The first few weeks I was with the club weren't too bad. I started hitting better, got a few home runs, and helped win a couple of ball games. Hodges really worked at making a first baseman out of me. What McGaha had done for me that day in spring training after I made all those errors against the Yankees, Hodges was doing every day.

In one way, he helped me more than McGaha had. Hodges had been an outstanding first baseman for the Dodgers for many years. He knew every trick of the trade. He taught me things about playing first base that most ballplayers never knew. I didn't like the guy and still was wary of him, but I appreciated his help. And I felt sort of sorry for him because we were in a terrible losing streak.

One night when I had dinner with one of the guys, I said, "Hodges is having a rough time. I wish we could do better for him."

The other guy, a good friend of mine, looked sharply at me and actually snarled, "Don't feel bad about Hodges. He's a no-good guy except when writers are around. He loves that ink, especially in New York."

"Well," I said, "he's treated me all right. And he hasn't shown any signs I could see of being a no-good guy to anyone else. I can't believe it until I see it."

"Wait," the other guy said. "You will."

We had been on the road about a week and were still in an awful losing streak when we arrived in New York. This was Gil Hodges' town. He had played there about ten years before the Dodgers moved to Los Angeles, his home was in Brooklyn, the writers were his buddies.

We had a meeting in the clubhouse before the game. Phil Ortega, scheduled to pitch, had missed the bus from the hotel to the ball park. John Orsino was on the disabled list and hadn't even been traveling with us. But he lived right outside of New York and, since he was home anyhow, he came to the ball park that night. He didn't have to and wasn't expected.

Well, the meeting was really something like I have never seen

155

before or since. All Hodges did was cuss guys out—one after another. He went from man to man, just giving hell to each one. Paul Casanova, the regular catcher, and Jim Hannan, one of our starting pitchers, had been having communication problems. Hannan, who was very nearsighted, could hardly make out the signs and, when he did see them, didn't like them and kept shaking them off.

I don't remember what Hodges said to Casanova, but Hannan sat right next to me. When Hodges reached him, he gave Jim a terrible going-over, ending it by saying, "The next time you shake off a sign from one of my catchers, you'll find yourself shaking off signs in the minors."

His eyes were blazing, and he was like a madman, he was so sore. He stopped in front of me but didn't say anything—there wasn't anything he could say. He knew I worked my ass off for him, and I was hitting pretty well.

Ortega walked in right in the middle of the meeting and started getting dressed. Hodges didn't see him at first. When he did, he turned and yelled, "Get that uniform off. We don't need you. Just get that uniform off and get the hell out of here."

Orsino walked in, just to visit—he wasn't even supposed to be there. Hodges whirled on him and said, "You're late. That'll cost you money." I heard later he fined Orsino a bundle.

Somebody started to say something about Orsino's being on the disabled list, but Hodges yelled, "Shut up. I'm running this ball club."

His eyes were still blazing, he was cussing to beat hell and, as I watched, I thought, *God, he's like a crazy man. What the hell's the matter with him? He throws a starting pitcher out, he fines a guy who just dropped in to help, he eats out Hannan for something that happened weeks ago.*

There was a knock on the door, and the clubhouse boy came over and said, "A couple of New York writers want to see you, Gil."

And suddenly this man who had been a raving maniac bawling out one man after another became a charmer. His face relaxed, his eyes softened, his voice changed as he said very quietly, "Send 'em in."

When the baseball writers walked in, Gil welcomed them like long-lost brothers. As he grinned and shook hands and slapped backs, one of them said, "Did we interrupt anything?"

"Oh, no," Hodges said. "We were just having a little meeting, talking a little baseball, getting a few things straight." Then, without another word to us, he turned and led them into his office.

I was floored. Never in my life had I seen a manager let anyone short of his own boss—his owner or general manager—stop a clubhouse meeting. And never had I seen a lion change to a lamb so fast.

The ballplayer who had told me about Hodges at dinner that night came over and said, "Remember what I told you? Remember I said he was a no-good guy?"

"Yup," I said.

"And remember that same night I said this guy loves publicity, particularly in New York?"

"Yup."

"And remember you said you were going to wait and see for yourself?"

"Yup."

"Well, have you seen?"

"I've seen," I said.

"You believe me now?"

"I'm weakening," I said. "He did a lot of things today that were pretty hard to take. But he still hasn't bothered me personally. I've got to take the guy as I find him."

"Give him time," the guy said. "He'll get around to you sooner or later."

It was sooner, but it happened in an odd, completely unexpected way. In the eighth or ninth inning of a close game at Minnesota, Zoilo Versalles of the Twins was on first base with one out when the hitter slammed a wicked shot down the first-base line which I made a great diving stop of. I was off balance—practically on my back, in fact—and the only play I had was to tag first and get the hitter. Instead, I tried for Versalles, a fast man, at second, and threw the ball away. It cost us the game.

I felt awful—so bad that when we got back to the hotel I phoned Hodges and asked if I could talk to him. I wanted to apologize for costing us the game. He told me to come on up. When I got there, he was in pajamas, ready for bed.

"I just want to tell you, Gil, how bad I feel about throwing away the game," I said.

"Don't feel bad," Hodges said. "That could happen to anyone. You made a great stop, and I was glad to see that. Your fielding is coming along fine."

I was there for maybe an hour, most of which was pleasant and relaxed. I did the talking, telling Gil how badly I wanted to help the club out of its misery, and he seemed to be sympathetic and grateful.

Then I said, "Isn't there something I could do to help snap us out of this slump? We're too good a ball club to be lousing things up so badly. Maybe I should start a fight. A good free-for-all might get us all pulling together."

Now, some managers would have jumped at the idea. Others might not go for it, but I'm sure they would say something like, "No, don't start a fight, but thanks for the offer. It shows how much you're willing to do to help."

But Hodges reacted in a way of his own. Without a word of appreciation, talking like a school principal to a recalcitrant kid, he said, "I don't want you to start a fight. This shows me something about what kind of a person you are."

158

Suddenly, the room felt as if an icy blast had just gone through it. The whole atmosphere changed so fast that I got up, thanked Hodges for listening, apologized for bothering him, and left. And from that night on, he never spoke another civil word to me.

The team slump finally eased off, and I was doing my share at the plate and in the field. As the weeks progressed, my hair, which I wore long anyhow, began to get a little shaggy, but that didn't affect my play. I continued to hit well, won a few ball games that helped pull us out of the cellar, and in general was feeling pretty good.

Except for an occasional ribbing from one of the other ballplayers, nobody mentioned the length of my hair. Since even I knew it was unusually long, I really intended to get it cut, but kept putting it off.

Then one day, as I went to the water cooler in the locker room for a drink, Hodges came over and said, "Don't come to the park tomorrow unless you get a haircut."

Taking it as a joke, I grinned and said, "All right, Gil."

He didn't grin back—just turned around and walked into his office. A couple of ballplayers standing there heard the exchange and one said, "That's what I like about our Gil—great sense of humor."

The next day Betty Ann wanted to take two of our kids to the doctor and I babysat with the other. She was back around three in the afternoon, giving me plenty of time for a haircut, but I didn't get around to it. I walked into the locker room at about five-thirty, got dressed for the game, and was heading for the trainer's room for some vitamin pills when Hodges came out of his office.

"Take your uniform off," he said. "You're not going to play. I told you to get a haircut yesterday. Why didn't you?"

"I couldn't," I said. "I had to babysit for one of my kids. I'll get a haircut tomorrow."

"You'll get one today or you won't play," Hodges said.

"It's too late," I said. "There isn't a barbershop open at this hour."

"That's none of my concern," Hodges said. "Get a haircut or take that uniform off."

"Gil, I'm hitting like hell and helping the ball club," I said. "You mean to say you'll bench me just because I need a haircut?"

"You heard me," he said. Then he went back into his office.

Boiling mad, I started cursing and bitching when Bobby Humphreys, who had been standing there, said, "Hey Hawk, I can cut hair."

"Will you cut mine?"

"Sure."

We went into the trainer's room and Bobby took scissors and a shaver and went to work. He gave me a horrible haircut—worst I ever had—but it counted. As soon as he finished, I went out to the field where Hodges had gone, walked up to him and said, "Is it O.K. for me to play now?"

He didn't crack a smile, just looked, and said, "Yeah."

I didn't get a hit that night, and got damn few hits the rest of the season. In fact, I went so bad that I spent a good part of September on the bench. And I don't remember exchanging a word with Hodges, not even a good-bye when the season ended.

The next spring—1967—when I reported to the Senators at Pompano Beach, Florida, we had three first basemen, Dick Nen, Bob Chance, and me. I didn't go to bat once in nearly two weeks. When the exhibition games began, Chance played most of the time and Nen the rest. I didn't even get to pinch-hit—just sat on the bench watching games, pitching batting practice and stuff like that.

Both Chance and Nen were pretty good ballplayers, but neither could hit or field with me, and Hodges knew it. But he didn't let me play until about two weeks before spring training ended. I hit the hell out of the ball, and Hodges started me every day, pulling me out in the late innings to give Nen some work. Chance was cut before we left Florida.

By the time we reached Washington I was the first baseman. One thing I wanted to do more than anything else was to play opening day, because the President and a sellout crowd always go to opening games in Washington. This would be my first, and I talked so much about what a thrill it would be that Hodges must have known how I felt.

I got a couple of hits in each of our last two exhibition games, against the Cardinals. By then, we all took the starting lineup for granted. With only an occasional exception, the same guys had been playing every day for a week. There wasn't a shadow of a doubt in my mind that I'd start against the Yankees on opening day. Although Mel Stottlemyre, their starting pitcher, was one of the best right-handers in the league, I had always hit him well enough and Hodges knew it.

I'm a pretty calm guy, but the morning of that opening day I was really juiced up. All opening days are a thrill anyhow, but this was something special—to play for the President of the United States. I was just about to take batting practice with the other regulars when Hodges posted the starting lineup on the wall. I glanced at it, then stared, hardly able to believe my eyes.

Dick Nen was playing first base.

As I turned away and shoved my bat into the batrack, Nen himself, a wonderful guy, very shy, very decent, came over and said, "Hawk, this is not right. I'm sorry I can't do anything."

"That's all right, Richard," I said.

Frank Howard, my roommate, said, "He must really hate your guts, Hawk. He knows how badly you wanted to play today."

Eddie Brinkman, Kenny McMullen, and maybe half a dozen others told me how sorry they were, and every one of them meant it. Just before the game, a Washington writer asked me, "What do you think about the lineup?"

"Well," I said, "he's making up the lineup card." I stopped, then moved away. I didn't want the writer to see the tears in my eyes.

When Hodges started me the second game of the season and kept me in almost every day after that, I knew he had benched me opening day just to hurt me. Any guy capable of pulling that dirty a trick was not for me. I was fed up with Gil Hodges. I had had all I could take of the man. I was so eager to get out from under him that I told the Washington writers for publication that I wanted to be traded.

"There's no sense kidding myself," I said. "I can't get along with Hodges. I want to go somewhere else."

Even Gil Hodges didn't want that kind of publicity. In New York he called me into his office and said, "Do you want to play for me?"

"I want to play baseball," I said.

"Why didn't you take batting practice that first day in Washington?" he said.

"I'll tell you why," I said. "I led the club in hitting and home runs just playing the last couple of weeks of spring training. I had a better spring than anyone else on the club. I should have started opening day. When I saw I wasn't going to, I was too disappointed to take batting practice."

"I know you should have started," Hodges said.

"Well, why didn't I?"

"Stottlemyre was pitching. Dick's a left-handed batter and a low-ball hitter."

"Stottlemyre's a great pitcher," I said, "but I've always hit him pretty well—and you know it."

At this point, I expected Hodges to blow his stack. Instead, he repeated, "You should have started. Now do you want to play ball for me or not?"

"I've got a job to do and you've got a job to do," I said. "It doesn't make any difference, I suppose, who I play for. But you don't like me, and I think you know that I don't like you. That shouldn't have anything to do with it. This is baseball. Personalities shouldn't enter into it. But they did on opening day. You knew how badly I wanted to play, but you kept me out because you don't like me."

"It's not that I don't like you," he said. "I just don't like some of the things you do."

"Well, Gil, I'm sorry," I said. "If you can get rid of me, I'd like to go to another ball club."

Then I walked out.

I thought, if nothing else, that talk would clear the air between us, but things got worse. Hodges criticized my hair, my clothes, my hats—everything but my baseball. One day I walked into the locker room wearing a little madras hat.

"Don't wear that any more," Hodges said.

Another time I got into a bus going from the hotel to the ball park—I think it was in Cleveland or New York—wearing a wild-looking madras sport jacket, with a white shirt, a blue tie, black slacks, and white shoes.

"Don't you think that looks pretty ridiculous?" Hodges said.

"I think it looks pretty neat," I said.

"Well, I don't," he said. "Don't wear that jacket again."

The most maddening thing about that was that at least two other guys were wearing almost exactly the same jacket and Hodges didn't say a word to either of them.

Although more and more unhappy with this guy, I was playing well. Since I had my stroke back and was hitting the ball hard, and fielding very well, I didn't have much hope of being traded. I figured if I could last the season without going nuts I'd be all right, because there were rumors even then that Hodges would leave Washington and manage the Mets when the 1967 season ended.

On June 9, having just arrived in Boston, Frank Howard and I were sitting in our room at the Sheraton Boston when the phone rang. It was Hodges, wanting to talk to me.

163

"Are you going to be in your room for a little while?" he said. He sounded friendly, almost humble.

"Yes," I said.

"Well, you're going to get a phone call."

"Do you mind if I ask what it's about?"

"I'd like to tell you, Hawk, but I can't," Hodges said. His voice was sugar sweet. He had never talked to me in friendlier tones.

"Look, Gil, if I'm going somewhere I'd appreciate your telling me."

He paused, then said, "O.K. I suppose there's no harm in telling you. Charley Finley's going to call you."

Half an hour later Finley called. He had bought me back from Washington for cash. I was going home to Kansas City, home to Alvin Dark, home to Charley Finley.

I couldn't have been happier.

12 | The Jolly Green Giant

If you happened to watch Frank Howard and me first meet after not having seen each other for a long time, you'd think we were both nuts. Conventional greetings are not for us. The ballplayers always call him Hondo, but I don't say, "Hello, Hondo, how the hell are you?" And he doesn't say, "Hi, Hawk, howya doing?"

We just peer at each other without saying anything for a few seconds. Then, without taking his eyes off me, he says, "So you're the fabulous Hawk, eh?"

And I say, as though accepting a challenge for a fight, "Yea-uh."

And he says, "What makes you so fabulous?"

And I say, "Because I can do it all."

This exchange is our standard greeting. Sometimes we don't even shake hands. We don't have to. Ever since we roomed together when I was with the Senators, we've been like blood brothers. We understand each other completely. This great big wonderful guy, six feet seven inches tall and 275 pounds of pure beef, was the best roommate I ever had, and, believe me, I've had some good ones.

It's such a pleasure to know that now he is not only one of base-ball's biggest stars but one of its highest paid. I know of no one

165

who deserves it more. He's the most powerful hitter in the game, its 1968 home-run king and, I'm sure, its home-run king for several years to come.

Rooming with Hondo almost made up for all the grief and problems I had playing for Gil Hodges. It's not often you have the pleasure of getting that close to one of nature's noblemen. I had more laughs, more real fun from my constant association with him than with any ballplayer I ever knew.

Hondo was like a teddy bear—friendly, good-natured, playful, generous. He never blew his stack. A man that big rarely has to. I have seen him momentarily sore, and that was enough. You could have fake fights with him, punch him around pretty hard, pull tricks on him, use him as the butt of practical jokes, but you could go only so far—and not one step farther.

One of our standard gags—Hondo's and mine—around the locker room was a phony boxing match. I'd put towels around my neck, the way a fighter does when he's heating up, and lash out at him, punching him in the chest or on the arms or shoulders, and he'd just stand there and grin. I might as well have been tickling him, for all the pain I inflicted.

I'm a pretty big guy myself—six-two and around 200 pounds—and I've knocked guys out with the kind of punches I threw in fun at Hondo. He could break me in half if he wanted to, but he never punched back, just took all I had to hand out. Then he would finally say, "Come on now, let's get into uniform. We've got to get to work, Fab."

He called me Fab because I called myself the fabulous Hawk. He was always saying, "We've got to get to work," but I never paid much attention. I'd just say, "Come on, big boy, I'm going to knock you right on your ass." Then we'd horse around a little longer before getting ready to go out on the field.

The one time he got sore at me he frightened me to death. We were having one of those boxing sessions, with me punching and

Hondo taking it, when I threw a pretty hard jab meant for his chest. Instead of standing still or turning to take the punch on his arm, or trying to fend me off, he ducked—and I caught him right on the nose.

That one hurt so much it brought tears to his eyes. He glared at me, and when I saw that look, I turned right around to run. He just reached out, grabbed me by the neck, pulled me back, and while holding me like a bug in one arm, reached with the other, picked me up and cradled me parallel to the ground.

"Hawk," he said, "I tell you, I'm tired of playing. Let's go to work."

Then, very gently, he put me down—and I went to work. As long as I live, I'll never forget that look in his eyes.

He has a hangup about people messing around with his clothes. Of course, his suits cost a fortune—they have to be made to order and they take as much material as for two ordinary guys. Even his slacks and shirts and sweaters are so expensive that he hates to wear them to the ball park. Instead, he often shows up in dungarees. He has maybe a dozen pairs of dungarees, just for the ball park.

One time he showed up about four days in a row in the same dungarees. When they began looking pretty raunchy, Eddie Brinkman, a skinny six-footer who loved to rib Hondo, looked at him in disgust and said, "You a major-league ballplayer? Did you ever hear of a fifty-thousand-dollar superstar coming to the ball park in damn dungarees?"

"What's wrong with dungarees?" Hondo said. "I've got to have something to relax in."

"Well, you don't have to relax in the same dungarees every day," Brinkman said.

As usual when on the receiving end of a ribbing, Hondo just grinned. When he was dressed and out to take batting practice, Brinkman went into the locker room and tied the dungarees all in

167

knots. Hondo came in to change his shirt, saw the knots, and looked around the room.

Then he said, "Boys, I don't know who did this, and I'm not going to ask. I'm just going to tell you one thing. I'm leaving the room for five minutes. Unless those dungarees are nicely straightened out and neatly hung up in my locker when I get back, I'm going to break every neck in this joint."

At the time, none of us knew Brinkman had done it—in fact, Eddie wasn't even in the room. None of us cared either. The minute Hondo walked out, about twenty-three guys rushed for his locker, beating each other's brains out to get those knots undone. And once we had done that, we even tried to press them—with a couple of guys stretching them out while a few more ran our hands up and down them.

We were still doing that when Hondo came back. He watched us for a minute and said, "Boys, I knew you would all come through for me. I knew none of you wanted to hurt me by tying my dungarees all up. I tell you, it's a great thing to have so many wonderful teammates."

Hondo wears false teeth—he has only about four of his own, all on top—and we were always ribbing him about his breath. It really isn't bad, but every time we got into a bus to go from the airport to the hotel or from the ball park to the airport, somebody would say, "Hondo, get off the bus—your breath is killing us."

One day Brinkman brought him one of those oversized toothbrushes, about a foot long. Hondo loved the thing. Every day after his shower he spent ten minutes scrubbing his false teeth with soap and water with that big toothbrush. But still there was always someone—usually Brinkman—who would say, "Hondo, you didn't brush enough. Your breath still smells terrible."

One night Hondo got some phony perfume—that stuff that smells like rotten eggs—and as he sat with us in the back of the bus, he kept yawning as though he were sleepy. With every yawn, he put a drop of his perfume into his mouth. The stuff takes a few seconds to work. Everytime he yawned he exhaled, and pretty soon this terrible smell permeated the whole back of the bus. It was the only time he really did have a terrible case of halitosis.

"Hondo," I said, "your damn breath smells worse than ever."

"You're kidding, Fab," he said. Then, sitting beside me, he almost knocked me out with a breath right at me.

"Hondo, for crissake," Brinkman yelled, "get off the damn bus before you smother us all."

"You're always kidding about my breath, Eddie," Hondo said. "You know it doesn't smell." Then he blew at Eddie.

I got up and moved up front, and Eddie followed me. Pretty soon Hondo had the whole back of the bus to himself. By the time we arrived at the ball park, everyone was rushing to get off ahead of him. He caught up with me, showed me his perfume, then dumped it into a barrel so he wouldn't louse up the whole locker room with it.

Actually, Hondo was very conscious of his breath. He carried Lavoris with him, and continually took swigs of it. He had his own way of using it. You're supposed to swish it around your mouth, gargle it, and spit it out. To Hondo, spit was a horrid word. He swished and he gargled, then he swallowed. I don't know how many of those bottles he went through a day, but he must have been the best customer Lavoris ever had.

The man was a fantastic eater, who loved every morsel and every drop that went down his huge gullet. During the spring, he was hitting like hell, winning ball games for us, and scaring the daylights out of opposing pitchers, which I would think would be just about all a manager could ask of a ballplayer. But he weighed about 280 pounds that year, and Hodges threatened to fine him if he didn't get down to 255 by the end of spring training.

This was like demanding I get a haircut. Hondo could no more see the necessity of losing weight when he was doing so well than

I could of a haircut. But when the boss told him to lose or it would cost him, he went on a monumental diet.

He practically fasted, eating one meal every two days. Outside of that the only things he had were orange juice, milk, and soft drinks. It was three or four miles from the hotel to the ball park, and Hondo ran each way every day. When he got so hungry he couldn't stand it he went to bed and tried to sleep it off.

By the time the season began, he was down to 255 all right, which saved the fine, but he was hitting like Little Miss Muffet. He looked thin and drawn, the bat was heavy in his hands, his swing was off, and he became a pushover for every pitcher he faced. More and more discouraged, he hit bottom one day when he struck out four times.

In the locker room he got dressed very slowly, didn't talk to anyone, didn't laugh at anything, and simply moped. Nobody ribbed him about his size or his breath or his clothes or anything. Even Brinkman stayed away from him. Hondo loved the guy and got a big kick out of everything Eddie did, but not then. Neither Eddie nor anyone else had dared say much to him for a couple of weeks.

Hondo and I always left the ball park together, and by then I was dawdling around every day waiting for him. After he was showered and dressed to leave—it was maybe four-thirty in the afternoon—Hondo said, "I've had it with this diet. Come on, Fab, let's go eat a sandwich or something."

There was a little restaurant and bar right near the ball park. After making sure that Hodges had gone, we went in there, and Hondo had five huge roast beef sandwiches, washing them down with six beers, not stopping even to take a breather. He ate all the sandwiches and drank all the beer faster than I could consume one sandwich and one beer.

He picked up the tab—he was always picking up tabs because he wouldn't let anyone spend a dime when he was around—and we took a cab to the hotel. He complained all the way of being hungry, and, as we sat around in the room, he griped and griped about Hodges' starving him to death. Finally, at about seven-thirty he gave up and got dressed. Then he said, "Come on, big guy. I'm going out and have me some kind of a meal. Let's go."

We didn't get any farther than the hotel dining room. After making sure the manager wasn't around. Hondo went to work on their buffet, which was really great. When he started around the long tables, he didn't even have a plate with him. He stopped, looked at a huge bowl of salad, took the big serving spoons and forks out of it, and carried it to the table. By the time I joined him, he had it half eaten, and pretty soon it was gone.

He went to the table and came back with a big platter with about everything the buffet offered on it: the biggest steak I ever saw, a tremendous chunk of fish, a whole chicken, God knows how many shrimp, and enough potatoes to feed a ball club. Then he went back for a pitcher of milk.

I looked at the platter and the pitcher, then looked at Hondo in absolute awe.

"Don't tell me you're going to eat all that," I said.

"I just hope it's enough," he said.

Too fascinated to eat, I simply watched. The steak was the first to disappear, then the fish, then the chicken. In between, he gobbled the shrimp and the potatoes and drank huge quantities of milk. When there was nothing but chicken bones left on the platter, Hondo stood up, and I said, "Where are you going?"

"Have to get some dessert," he said.

He came back with a whole apple pie, eating it in just about the time it took me to eat one piece. Then we went up to the room to watch television.

At about ten-thirty, Hondo said, "Let's have a few beers," so we went to a little bar and restaurant where the ballplayers hung out.

Curfew was midnight, and Hondo had maybe half a dozen beers while I was drinking two. When the clock on the wall said eleven-thirty, Hondo said, "Man, I'm hungry. We've just got time for a bite to eat."

The restaurant part of this joint was a patio in back. The two of us went to a table there, and he ordered a fourteen-ounce steak and a dozen scrambled eggs.

The waitress, whom we all knew, turned to me and said, "What'll you have, Hawk?"

"Honey," I said, "I'll get full just watching Hondo."

He polished off the steak and eggs in plenty of time for us to make the curfew.

Just before we went to bed Hondo said, "Hey, we forgot to order breakfast."

"O.K.," I said, "I'll call room service. You want your usual glass of milk?" That was all he had been having for breakfast since starting his diet.

"No," he said, "after you've ordered, let me talk to the girl."

I ordered my usual—orange juice, steak, and a couple of eggs, an order of toast and some milk and Hondo took the phone.

"I want a quart of orange juice," he said, "a quart of milk, the biggest steak you've got, and a dozen scrambled eggs." He paused, then added, "And don't forget toast—lots of toast."

When I finished breakfast the next morning I just sat and watched while Hondo cleaned the plate. And that afternoon he had his best day of the year—a couple of home runs and a double, I think it was.

Because he had picked up so many of my tabs in so many places, I wanted to take him out, but he kept refusing. Finally, when we were in Baltimore one night, Betty Ann drove up from Washington for a couple of days before we went west on a long road trip. She liked Hondo and thought it was a great idea when I suggested we take him to dinner at Brooks Robinson's restaurant.

As we dressed at the ball park after the game, I said, "Remember, Hondo, this is my tab."

"We'll see after we get there," he said.

"No sir, big guy," I said. "I'm paying or we don't go. If I don't, Betty Ann will be insulted."

"O.K., O.K.," he said. "I don't want to hurt your wife's feelings."

When the three of us sat down in the restaurant, I said, "What do you want to start with?"

"A little beer," he said.

While I was having two, Hondo had six. I think Betty Ann had a martini or something, but she didn't pay much attention to it. She was too busy watching Hondo gulp the beers down like water.

I ordered three salads, but, as the waitress turned to leave, Hondo said, "What kind of bowls do you have back there?"

The waitress looked at him in a funny way, and I said, "Bowls? Bowls? What are you talking about, Hondo? You know what a salad bowl looks like."

"Miss," Hondo said, "I don't want those little things you've got. Don't you have big salad bowls?"

"You mean the kind for five or six people?" she said.

"That's right," Hondo said. "Bring me one of those."

After the salad, Hondo ordered an eighteen-ounce steak—the biggest they served. Betty Ann asked for a six-ounce filet, and I wanted a fourteen-ounce steak. While we were waiting for the steaks, Hondo noticed that Betty Ann, who is a very small eater, had left half her salad.

"Aren't you going to finish it?" he said.

"No, I've had enough," Betty Ann said.

"Mind if I do?"

"Not at all."

So Hondo polished off her salad. When the steaks came, he finished his in a hurry. I couldn't eat more than half of mine, and Betty Ann didn't have more than two or three bites of hers. Hondo

173

looked at our plates and said, "Is that all you're having?" When we both nodded, he swapped plates with me, finished my steak, then swapped with Betty Ann and finished hers.

"What'll you have for dessert?" I said. "Pie, or cake, or ice cream or something?"

"I'm not having any dessert," Hondo said. "I'm on a diet."

Hondo roomed with me at that 1967 LaCosta tournament in San Diego. I had a buddy from Savannah in the navy there—a guy named Jerome Henry—who had just got married. He phoned to ask if he could bring his wife and another couple up to see me. I told him to come on up but neglected to say I had a roommate and neglected to tell Hondo they were coming.

When the two couples arrived at about nine in the evening, Hondo was taking a nap. The five of us were having a drink in the kitchen when Hondo woke up. Before I had a chance to warn him, he came strolling in from the bedroom in his shorts.

Hondo is a sight to behold under any circumstances. It isn't just his height—I know a lot of guys six-seven and over—nor his weight —I know plenty of football players around 275. It's the whole ensemble that gets you. He's just big all over, and at LaCosta he was bigger than usual—must have weighed 300 pounds.

As he came walking in, yawning and stretching, all these people could see was a practically naked monster with only four widely spaced upper teeth showing. He was rubbing his eyes as he mumbled, "Come on, Fab, let's get something to eat." Without his choppers, his speech was a confused grunt and he looked like a gigantic blond ape straight out of the jungle. He would have scared his own grandmother.

When he saw I had company, he turned and ran back to the bedroom to put on some clothes. At the same time, Jerome, who stands about five-three and weighs 110 pounds soaking wet, took one look at this monstrous, mumbling apparition and ran out the door so fast that I had to chase him all the way to the thirteenth green before I caught him. I never saw a guy so scared. He thought Hondo was a giant maniac who had come in to kill us all.

Halfway through the 1968 season, Hondo and I were in a battle for the American League slugging honors. When the Senators came to Boston, I was about twenty runs-batted-in ahead of him and he was leading me by three home runs. The Senators had come into town late and we didn't meet until we were on the field.

Hondo walked over to me and, as we peered at each other, he said, "So you're the fabulous Hawk, eh?"

"Yea-uh," I said.

"What makes you so fabulous?"

"Because I can do it all," I said.

He grinned, then said, "Y'know, Fab, I hope you hit fifty home runs . . ."

"Thanks, Hondo," I said. "That's very decent of you."

". . . As long as I hit fifty-one," he said.

13 | Finley's Folly

When I walked into the Kansas City ball park the day after the Senators sold me back to the Athletics, Alvin Dark and I practically fell into each other's arms. After talking a while, he said, "O.K., Hawk, I'm going to let you watch a couple of ball games. I know what you've been through with Hodges, and I want you to clear your mind. You're an emotional guy, but now it's all over. I know you and you know me, and now everything is going to be all right. I watched you whenever we played Washington, and I know you've got your stroke back. You're ready to break loose at the plate and really help us."

I sat on the bench for three or four games, pinch-hit a couple of times and hit the ball hard. Then one day Alvin said, "Are you ready?"

"I'm all set, Alvin."

"O.K. From now on, you're my first baseman."

Alvin moved Ramon Webster from first base to the outfield, and life looked rosy to us all. We were pulling together, winning our share of games and, although fiddling around the cellar, had a shot at eighth or seventh place.

I was going crazy at the plate—just belting the hell out of the ball. I went to Kansas City with a .200 average in early June and by mid-August I was hitting .285. That eighty-five point difference meant that I had been hitting .315 in the two and a half months since returning from Washington.

Since Betty Ann and I hadn't sold our Kansas City house and the people we leased it to happened to move out when I returned there, we just went right back in. Everything was great, or almost everything.

Now that I was back on his ball club, Finley started taking money out of my salary again. I don't really know how much I owed him—maybe five or six thousand—and he took huge bites from my checks. It got so bad that I found myself working at half pay. On the first and fifteenth of the month, Finley was milking me dry. Sometimes I got as little as a hundred and fifty dollars, and I had to call my mama for financial help. Since Alvin didn't want me doing anything to take my mind off baseball, I didn't play golf, didn't play pool, didn't gamble—just struggled along.

It got so bad that Alvin went to Finley and begged him to let me keep what I was earning.

"The kid's going great guns," Alvin said. "You'll probably be giving him a big raise anyhow. Why can't you let him alone for now?"

But Finley flatly refused. I guess he felt I had to make up for the money he hadn't collected while I was with Washington.

Although worried about finances, I was hitting so well that I led the club in just about everything. In July and August, the only man in the league doing better was Carl Yastrzemski, who was in the process of pacing the Red Sox to their surprise pennant.

There was one other little cloud in the silver lining. Alvin Dark and Finley weren't getting along too well. They continued to argue over little things, just as they had before, and I got the idea that Charley was getting ready to change managers again. Alvin was finishing his second season and Charley rarely kept anyone around that long.

Then, without warning, we were all suddenly involved in the most bizarre incident of the year. It started with an airplane ride from Boston to Kansas City on August 3, at the end of a long road trip. We were six and six for the trip, finishing up by beating the Red Sox two out of three in Boston. I won both games, one with a homer off Gary Bell, the other with a double off Johnny Wyatt.

In the only game we lost Jack Aker got bombed, and, as we were about to board the plane back to Kansas City, I grabbed him and said, "Come on, big guy, let's you and me sit in back and talk about your pitching."

"O.K.," Aker said.

He followed me down the aisle to the very last two seats on the plane. As usual, we traveled commercially, because Finley wouldn't spend the dough for a charter. He saved fifty thousand dollars a year while costing us maybe two dozen ball games. We spent so many hours around airports waiting for regular flights to take off that we were often too pooped to play by the time we arrived where we were going. Almost every other club in the two leagues flew by charter, and a couple had airplanes of their own.

Aker, our player representative, was a very quiet guy under the best of conditions. Now, still down after the beating he had taken, he was quieter than ever. Not much of a drinker or heller-arounder, he lived for baseball, always kept in shape, and never got into trouble. But he was so tense and upset I insisted he have a few belts, knowing they'd relax him. The times I had seen him drink I noticed it had hardly any effect on him. Rather than make him exuberant, loud, violent, or anything like that, it made him quieter than ever.

Liquor also tends to quiet me down. I'm naturally a bubbling, happy sort of guy, enjoy life to the full, and don't ever get a real buzz on. The worst that happens to me is what happened during

Jack Haley's crazy golf tournament in Kansas City. I lose my co-ordination and get sleepy, but never violent or loud.

I bring these points out because what happened later made it appear that Aker and I were among the guys who were supposed to have got drunk and obnoxious and loud on that particular flight. The plane stopped in Baltimore and St. Louis en route to Kansas City. Some of us had drinks, but not one guy did one thing that would in any way reflect discredit on the ball club. I know, because, sitting in the very back, I was one of the few who could see the length of the plane. If anyone had made unusual noise or acted drunk or caused trouble, I would have seen it.

Neither Aker nor I left our seats all the way to Kansas City. I did the talking, telling him he was too good a pitcher to let an occasional bad job worry him. I talked about his great sinker and his slider and suggested he change speeds a little more often. He just nodded, but I knew he was taking it all in. He told me later how much he appreciated my talking as I did.

Meanwhile, the stewardesses were walking up and down the aisle, passing out miniature bottles of booze. We had only one drink between Boston and Baltimore, and maybe five or six more the rest of the way to Kansas City. Liquor on airplanes is supposed to be confined to two to a customer, but several of our guys who didn't drink gave us theirs. We didn't ask for any extras—the girls just brought them and said, "This is So-and-so's. He doesn't drink." The more we drank, the quieter we acted. Each time a stewardess saw us with an empty glass and brought along a refill, we thanked her, she told us we were welcome, and that was the extent of our conversation.

Lew Krausse was sitting right in front of us. Mike Hershberger, my roommate, Danny Cater, and Jim Gosger were near by. None had more than two drinks, if that. A few guys up forward had one or two, but nobody drank heavily. And everyone behaved well. I didn't even hear a voice raised. There was no yelling back and forth, no monkeying around with the stewardesses, no unsolicited conversation with other passengers, nothing that anyone had to be ashamed of.

Alvin Dark, who doesn't drink, was up front playing bridge with three of the coaches. He rarely came back to check on the ballplayers because he knew it wasn't necessary. I don't remember a single trip—and certainly not that one—in which anyone did anything requiring disciplinary action on his or anyone else's part.

Somebody—I truly don't know who, although I read a magazine report that it was Monte Moore, the club's broadcaster—apparently got word to Dark that there was a lot of trouble in the back of the plane generated by ballplayers' drinking too much. It might have been Moore, it might have been somebody else connected with the club, or it might have been a passenger.

A good many of the ballplayers thought it was Moore because they didn't like him. They called him Monte the Ripper, since he often put the slug on guys during his broadcasts. Since we didn't hear him very much because we were on the field or in the dugout, you couldn't prove it by us.

Anyhow, Dark came back to see what was going on, which was nothing. When Alvin asked me how things were, I thought he meant how Aker was doing, because he knew how unhappy Jack was getting on the plane. After I told him we were fine, he left, stopping to talk to ballplayers as he returned to his own seat up front. I think he might have talked to the stewardesses, too, and perhaps even a few passengers. I know that everyone he approached assured him everything was quiet.

The stewardesses were wonderful. One, in fact, went through all the steaks to find a well done one for me because I don't like steaks rare. The girls went out of their way to see that we had everything we wanted and were comfortable. And on our part, we acted like

perfect gentlemen, as the stewardesses would gladly have told anyone who might have bothered to check with them. (Outside of
Dark, I doubt if anyone connected with the Athletics did.)

We were so pleased at their treatment of us that we drew up a
letter addressed to TWA's president, reporting on the great job
they did for us during the flight. Fifteen or twenty guys signed it,
and we mailed it when we got to Kansas City.

It appeared to be just a routine plane flight for everybody. I
don't think anyone had as much to drink as Aker and me, and nobody was loaded. None of us staggered off or in any way appeared
to be stiff. There were some wives waiting for us at the airport who
saw us get off. They didn't think anyone acted unusual, and nobody
—not a single one of us—showed the least evidence of having had
too much. In a flight of that distance, with the drinking broken up
by a steak dinner, how smashed can you get?

On August 18 we flew to Washington to begin a road trip with
a night game there. As we went aboard the plane, Alvin said,
"We're not going to have any drinks on the flight." He didn't explain why and nobody asked. We didn't think much about it one
way or the other because we often flew on planes where no liquor
was served.

But when we reached Washington, we were stunned to learn
that Finley had suspended Lew Krausse and fined him five hundred
dollars for "being drunk and disorderly" on the return flight from
Boston August 3. Why Finley waited so long or why he picked on
Krausse is something I'll never know. If I ever heard of a bum rap,
this was it. I knew Krausse hadn't had more than two drinks, because he sat right in front of me. And he certainly was neither
drunk nor disorderly.

If there was more to it than what I saw with my own eyes, I
never learned what it was. If Krausse did anything at all anywhere
and under any conditions that warranted such a stiff penalty, I'm
damned if I know what that was either. Maybe Finley used the

flight to cover up something else. But Krausse, one of the nicest guys on the team and a close friend of mine since our rookie days in Olean, would never do anything I can think of that was worth a suspension and a five-hundred-buck fine.

Krausse's penance for whatever the hell he did or Finley thought he did was only the first of a series of bombshells dropped by Finley. When we arrived at the stadium, Aker, as our player representative, called a locker-room meeting and told us Finley had ordered him to read us the following statement:

> To the members of the Kansas City Athletics:
> Effective immediately and for the balance of the season, all alcoholic drinks will no longer be served on commercial airlines to members of the Kansas City Athletics.
> The Kansas City Athletics will no longer tolerate the "shenanigans" of a very few individuals who obviously do not appreciate the privilege of playing in the major leagues and being treated like gentlemen.
> The attitude, actions and words of some of you have been deplorable.
> As a member of Organized Baseball you have certain responsibilities and obligations to yourself, your family, your club and most important of all—the fans.
> To the vast majority of you who have always conducted yourselves as gentlemen on and off the playing field, I sincerely regret the necessity of this action.
> Sincerely,
> Charles O. Finley

As I recall, Dark was not in the room, although I may be wrong. We had so many damn meetings and indignation sessions that I don't remember when Alvin was there and when he wasn't. I definitely recall Aker, who was as mad as the rest of us, telling us that Finley had said he would release the statement to the press, in the face of Aker's objections.

We immediately decided that Aker should call Finley back and demand that he keep the statement out of the papers and retract the obvious implication that we were a bunch of drunks who didn't know how to behave in public. But when Jack phoned Finley, it was too late. Charley had already released the statement and, in fact, it was all over the Washington sports pages that night.

The next day, after several meetings in various guys' rooms, we drew up a statement of our own. Aker wrote most of it, but half a dozen others, including me, helped. It read:

> In response to Charles O. Finley's statement of August 18, we, the players of the Kansas City Athletics, feel that an unjust amount of pressure has been brought to bear on several members of the club who had no part whatsoever in the so-called incident on the recent plane trip between Boston and Kansas City.
>
> The overwhelming opinion of the players is that the entire matter was blown out of proportion. Mr. Finley's policy of using certain unauthorized personnel in his organization as go-betweens has led to similar misunderstandings in the past and has tended to undermine the morale of the club. We players feel that if Mr. Finley would give his fine coaching staff and excellent manager the authority they deserve, these problems would not exist.

Every player except Rick Monday, who was on duty with the Marine Corps, signed the statement.

A couple of us, including Aker and me, took it up to Alvin Dark's room, let him read it, and told him we were releasing it to the press. He grinned and said, "If you do, you're going to get me fired. But if that's what you guys want to do, go right ahead."

"Alvin," Aker said, "we feel this is the thing to do. We're going to issue the statement to the press."

"If that's the way you feel," he said, "don't let me stop you. Finley will fire me sooner or later anyhow."

There was hell to pay when the statement came out. Finley

phoned Aker and demanded a retraction. Aker said he'd take a poll of the club, and that if we voted to retract we'd retract. He called another meeting, and we voted unanimously to stick by the statement. Although we didn't know it, Finley was already on his way to Washington.

I don't know when he arrived, but it must have been long after the night game ended, because he phoned Alvin at one-thirty in the morning for a huddle among various people connected with the club. Since I wasn't one of them, I know the curious sequence of events only from what I was told later.

The boys apparently had a busy night. Among those present besides Finley and Dark were Eddie Lopat (then a front-office executive), Eddie Hurley, the traveling secretary, Monte Moore, and a couple of coaches. Finley wanted Jack Aker there, too, but Aker picked that night as one of his few to miss curfew. That, of course, fixed him up real good with Finley when he finally did show up, but had no effect on the eventual outcome.

The meeting lasted three hours and must have been a beaut. As I understand it, Finley began by firing Alvin for, as Finley put it, "losing control of his ball club." This was ridiculous. Alvin was in full control. I never had a manager more respected by his players or in better control of them. We all would gladly have gone to hell and back for him.

Some time during the night, after Dark had assured Finley that the Athletics could win the pennant by 1971 or sooner with their promising young team, Charley did a complete about-face by offering Dark a two-year contract with a nice salary raise. Alvin, fired and rehired, went to bed a happy man at four-thirty in the morning.

His happiness lasted exactly one hour, because at five-thirty Finley phoned Alvin and fired him again. The reason he gave was that Aker had told him Alvin had seen the players' statement before we released it. There certainly was no secret about that, but Finley claimed Alvin had previously told him he hadn't seen the statement

185

in advance. Alvin told me otherwise. In any event, by the time we woke up in the morning, the interim manager was Luke Appling, one of the coaches.

Appling was a nice guy whom we all liked, but we were so stunned about Dark that we hardly appreciated how ridiculous the whole situation was. Alvin had set a new record for managers' being fired in one night, and Finley for owners' changing their minds. Everybody, including Alvin, can laugh as we look back on it today, but at the time it was pretty damn serious.

Finley had made Alvin the fall guy while converting a molehill into a mountain. The ballplayers were completely confused. We wanted Alvin back, but we knew a petition for his return would simply make matters worse. Finley wouldn't change his mind again and we would put Appling in an untenable position. All we could do was gripe and bitch in the bus on the way to the stadium for a scheduled afternoon game and in the locker room after we got there.

The game was rained out. While we waited in the clubhouse, Alvin dropped in to say good-by. He started to make a little speech but didn't get much of it out. After a sentence or two, his eyes filled with tears, and so did ours. Alvin stopped trying to talk, went around wordlessly shaking hands with us individually, and left.

Since I was closer to Alvin than anyone else on the ball club, the thing hit me hardest of all. I'm a pretty emotional guy and was openly crying when Alvin walked out. Here this wonderful guy and truly great manager had been the victim of one of the rawest deals I had ever seen. His only thought had been for the ball club, and all he got for his loyalty to it was a kick in the teeth.

Before we left Washington, half a dozen newspapermen came in to get our reactions to what had happened. I was in a fog—really so shook I shouldn't have said anything. There were tears in my eyes, I could hardly talk, and all these guys were crowding around asking for public statements from the ballplayers. When a writer came to me, all I could think of was what Finley had done, not only to Alvin, but to the whole club. Because of something that never happened on an airplane trip nearly three weeks before, he had made a fool of himself, a scapegoat of Krausse, alleged drunks out of us, and an apparently ineffectual manager out of Dark.

"The only thing I know," I said, "is that Charley Finley's actions of the last few days have been bad for baseball. I think they have been detrimental to the game."

I thought no more about it as we got into street clothes, packed our bags, and boarded a bus for Baltimore, where we had a game the following night. After dinner, there was a lot of visiting back and forth among the ballplayers in the hotel, guys just drifting into each other's rooms to talk about the developments and speculate about the future.

Finally, Mike Hershberger and I were alone in our room. Both emotionally and physically exhausted, we were too tired to go downstairs for a sandwich, so we called the bellhop to bring us a couple. We sat on our beds eating and watching television, when another bombshell broke.

A sports announcer I had known at Binghamton, John Kennelly, who was giving scores and other news, finished his broadcast by saying, "How's this for a quote from an employee about the boss who pays his salary? After Finley fired Dark, first baseman Ken Harrelson of the Kansas City Athletics, said that Finley was a menace to baseball."

Right away Hershberger fell off his bed laughing. He thought it was funny, but I was scared to death. I *knew* I hadn't called Finley a menace, but I realized how the guy interviewing me could have said I had. After all, he had his hands full taking notes from every ballplayer he could interview, and it would have been easy enough for him to use "menace" for "detrimental" when he wrote his story.

I wasn't afraid of what Charley could do to hurt me. I simply knew that the minute that quote got to him he'd raise a justifiable stink. I didn't know what form the stink would take—I was only sure there would be one. He wouldn't take anything like that from one of his own ballplayers.

Other guys who had seen the same television program began drifting into the room—Lew Krausse, Cotton Nash, Catfish Hunter, Jack Aker, Jim Gosger—maybe a dozen in all. Of course, the first thing they asked was had I really called Finley a menace. I told them I hadn't. Some, like Hershberger, thought it was funny. Others figured I'd be disciplined in some way—fined, maybe suspended—and still others thought Finley would be satisfied if I retracted the statement, or at least the "menace" part.

All I knew was that every baseball fan in the country would *think* I had called Finley a menace. While the guys milled around in the room, I phoned Betty Ann in Kansas City and said, "Look, something happened tonight and I know there'll be repercussions, but don't worry. I was misquoted in the papers, but everything's going to be all right. I'm sure the worst that will happen to me will be a fine. I'm not going to take any phone calls, so don't try to reach me. I'll get in touch with you tomorrow."

After phoning my mama in Savannah to give her the same message, I told the hotel operator, "I don't want any calls. I'm unavailable, no matter who tries to reach me. I just want to leave a call for ten in the morning."

We sat around yakking with the gang for maybe a couple of hours. Finally—it must have been after two in the morning—we were all too exhausted to stay up any longer. The boys left, and Mike and I went to bed.

14 | Hitting the Jackpot

The phone jangled me out of a troubled sleep. I reached for it with my eyes closed, thinking, *Gawd, it got to be ten o'clock quick.* I didn't want to talk to anybody. All I wanted to do was sleep.

"What time is it?" I grunted.

"Nine o'clock," the operator said. "I think it's your wife."

I sat up straight. It must be an emergency, I thought. Maybe one of the kids was sick.

"Put her on," I said.

The next voice I heard was not my wife's. It wasn't even a woman's.

"Kenny, this is Charley. Did you make those statements in the papers?"

"I didn't call you a menace. I did say everything else."

"Kenny, I've done you a lot of favors."

"You hurt me a few times, too," I said.

"I've been good to you," Finley said. "Now I want you to write a public retraction and give it to the papers."

As we talked, Mike sat up in the next bed, then, without asking, got up, threw on a pair of pants and a shirt, and left the room. When the door closed, I said, "Charley, I'll be glad to retract the word 'menace,' but I won't retract anything else."

"That's not good enough," Finley said, his voice rising. "I've got to have a public retraction of the whole statement."

"I'll retract the 'menace,' " I said again, "because I never said it. But that's all I'll retract."

Finley blew his stack. For about five minutes he screamed into the phone, yammering so fast that he became incoherent. When he calmed down he said, "Kenny, I'm going to send you to Birmingham."

"No, you're not," I said. "You're not going to send me to Birmingham. You can't send me out of this league."

"I'm going to try," he said. "I'm going to suspend you."

"That's up to you," I said.

"What do you want?" he demanded, his voice rising again. "You want your release?"

"No, Charley, I don't want my release," I said. "If you give me my release I might have trouble getting another job. Besides, I like Kansas City. I like the town. I like the fans." I meant it.

"I'll call you back in half an hour," Finley said, before hanging up.

I didn't move. Just sat up in bed.

What can the guy do? I thought. *Suspend me? For what? He'd just be cutting off his nose to spite his face. I'm the second best hitter in the American League. I'm killing the ball. No, he won't suspend me. Fine me maybe. But not suspend me.*

The possibility that he might fire me never occurred to me.

Fifteen or twenty minutes went by, with me sitting there, wondering what was going to happen next. Then the phone rang again.

"Kenny?"

"Yeah."

"Charley."

His voice was hard, and he talked as if he were reciting a legal paper or something.

"As of this moment," he said, "you have your unconditional release from the Kansas City Athletics. As of this moment, you are no longer a member of the Kansas City Athletics."

Then he hung up.

I was stunned. I couldn't believe my ears. I had been fired—me, the second best hitter in the American League, thrown out like a piece of trash. Yet this should be good—this should be great—this should be wonderful—

But I didn't fell good or great or wonderful. I was scared to death.

No owner would fire a hitter like me—just like that, I thought. No owner would dump a piece of property he could sell for six figures. It's impossible—far out—out of sight—unheard of. There's got to be a hitch—a gimmick. What can it be? Charley's sore. He wants to hurt me. And he can't hurt me by giving me my release— not with four American League teams, any one of which can use a hot hitter, scrambling for the pennant. They'd be willing to spend a fortune for me. If Charley Finley wanted to sell me, he could get all that money. By firing me, he put me in a spot where I can get it. I can sell my services to the highest bidder. He can't mean for me to do that. There must be something wrong somewhere.

I stretched and rubbed my eyes, trying to clear my head. I began thinking about Kansas City, and how Betty Ann and I loved the town, and about the nice little house we had there which Charley Finley helped me buy, and about my friends there, and the wonderful fans. I felt tears coming, and blinked to keep them back. They came again as a sudden horrible thought occurred to me.

Of course! I thought. Finley's going to get me blacklisted. No team in baseball will take me after this. Who wants a ballplayer who calls his owner a detriment? A detriment? They all think I called Charley a menace. And I'll bet he's phoning every other owner right now to make sure nobody takes me. I won't be able to get a job. Here I am, the second best hitter in the league, with no-body to play for.

By the time Hershberger came back, I was so busy feeling sorry for myself I hardly noticed him.

"What happened, Hawk?"

"I just got released," I said.

"You lucky sonofabitch! You lucky, lucky sonofabitch!"

He jumped up and down, whacked me on the back, bounced on the bed, and yelled and yelled and yelled.

"You lucky sonofabitch, you! It could only happen to you. Not me. You! I'd pay for my release. You get yours for nothing. Chee-zuz Kee-rist!"

"Maybe he had me blacklisted," I said.

"Blacklisted, my ass!" Hershberger said. "How can he get you blacklisted? Man, hitting like you're hitting, you're about to make one quarter of a million bucks. You've got it made. Made!"

There was a knock on the door and Catfish Hunter walked in with a couple of other guys.

"Hey," Hershberger howled. "What do you think? The Hawk got his release. Finley fired him!"

They all started jumping around, yelling about my luck and how much they envied me and why the hell couldn't it have happened to them, but I still couldn't believe that everything was all that good. Then the phone rang.

"Mr. Ken Harrelson?"

"Yeah."

"Just a minute for Mr. Short."

Eddie Short was general manager of the Chicago White Sox, who were in a death struggle for the pennant with the Detroit Tigers, the Minnesota Twins, and the Boston Red Sox. Of the four contending clubs, the White Sox were hurting the most for hitters.

"I understand you and Charley had a little problem," Short said.

"Yeah."

"He put you on the irrevocable waiver list."

"I didn't know that," I said.

Hell, I didn't even know there was an irrevocable waiver list. The only waiver list I ever heard of was the regular one, where a guy's name can be withdrawn any time a club feels like withdrawing it. I found out later that the club can't do that when it puts somebody on the irrevocable waiver list. After four days the player gets his outright release and can sign with anyone. The only person who can take him off the irrevocable list is himself. As far as Charley Finley was concerned, I was beyond reach.

Unless, say, Charley called me that afternoon and said, "Kenny, look. I was mad. I lost my temper. Come on back. I'll give you a nice raise. I'm sorry this happened, and I'm sure you are, too." Maybe he could talk me into going back. Then I would just call the league office and say, "I want to be taken off the irrevocable waiver list and go back on the Kansas City roster," and that would be the end of it.

But Charley didn't call. If he had, I'd have gone back.

Anyhow, Eddie Short said, "We'd like to have you in Chicago. You're all we need to nail down the pennant."

I said, "Well—" and stopped. I didn't know what to say, and Short knew it.

"What do you think about money?" he said.

What did I think about money? Mike Hershberger had said I'd make a quarter of a million dollars. But that was too much. I couldn't ask for that. What could I ask for? Whenever you're in a spot like that, it's a thousand-to-one you'll undersell yourself. I had been underselling myself all my life.

Like when I was a kid, cutting grass. I'd ask for a dollar when I could have got a buck and a half, a buck seventy-five. I'd do ten lawns a day, putting the price up every time. I'd collect one seventy-five for the last lawn when I should have collected that for each. It was a simple lesson in economics I never really learned. All the time I was growing up I never had the nerve to ask one seventy-five of my first customer—only the last.

So here's a guy asking me what I want and I'm afraid to tell him. If I say a hundred thousand and he takes it, I'll kick myself for not asking twice as much. But what if he comes back with something less? Do I say yes, or no? Do I stall? Will I get an offer from somebody else?

"Give me some idea what you want," Short said. "Then we'll make you an offer and stick to it."

"I have to think it over," I said.

"O.K.," Short said. "I'll tell you this, though. We're not going to get into a bidding contest. You'll make a lot of money out of this—there's no doubt about that. But bidding contests are bad for everyone—for you, for us, for baseball. Now how much do you think you're worth?"

"A hundred thousand?" I said.

It was a question, not a demand. How the hell did I know how much I was worth?

Short didn't say yes and he didn't say no. All he said was to call him again before I signed with anyone else, and I said I would.

When I hung up, Hershberger, lying on his bed chortling and making faces, said, "Gawd, you're a twelve-thousand-dollar-a-year ballplayer and you're up to your ass in debt and all of a sudden you come out with a hundred grand and play it cool. Hawk—I love you. I'm proud of you. Let me be your agent."

"I have to check," I said. "I can't believe this yet."

So I phoned Charley Segar in the baseball commissioner's office in New York, but he was out and I got his secretary.

"This is Ken Harrelson," I said. "I hear I'm on some waiver list. Would you please tell me exactly where I stand?"

After asking me to hold the line, she came back and said, "You're on the irrevocable waiver list."

"What does that mean to me?"

"It means Mr. Finley can't withdraw your name."

"Does it mean if he wants me back he can't get me back?" I said.

"That's exactly what it means. There's no way Charley Finley can get you back if you don't want to go back."

"Then I'm a free agent?"

"You will be after four days," she said.

I made her repeat it all about five times. She was very sweet and very patient, and I could have kissed her. Because when I hung up I finally knew I wasn't dreaming. Especially when the phone rang again.

"Mr. Harrelson?"

"Yes."

"This is Calvin Griffith's secretary in Minnesota. Mr. Griffith's been trying to get you but your line was busy. Will you be there when he returns from lunch?"

"I'll be here," I said.

After that the phone never stopped ringing. The hotel operator told me at one point I had three long-distance calls stacked up. I remember thinking that news travels awfully fast when the second best hitter in the league suddenly gets sprung from his ball club.

But I don't remember exactly who else called or in what order. There was so much confusion it was hard to talk. The traffic in the room was pretty heavy, with guys coming in and out all the time and Hershberger pointing at me on the phone and yelling dollar signs all over the place.

The only call I made myself was to my wife in Kansas City. She hadn't read the papers, so when I first told her I was released she burst into tears. She got over that fast after I explained the situation. I told her I'd be home the next day.

With all the phone calls, I didn't get a single firm offer. Everyone said the same thing—don't sign with anyone until you talk to us. I guess the only reason ball clubs call ballplayers is to tell them they'll talk to them later.

195

One guy who didn't call—at least while I was still in the room—was Calvin Griffith. Maybe he had a late lunch or maybe he couldn't reach me. Anyhow, I never did get to talk to him until I got back to Kansas City.

Just before I went downstairs to eat with the guys, Haywood Sullivan phoned. He was the player personnel director of the Red Sox and an old friend of mine. We had played together at Kansas City, and he later managed me there.

"Are you going to be in Baltimore tonight?" he said.

When I said I would, he said, "I'm coming down to talk to you. Let's meet where nobody will bother us."

"How about the airport?" I said. "We can talk over a beer or something."

He told me what plane he'd be on, and then I went down to join the gang. On the way through the lobby I bought one of those foot-long dollar cigars, and walked into the dining room twirling it around like a baton. Later, I took a cab to the ball park. I had to go there to pick up my gear, which had been shipped in with the rest of the equipment from Washington, where we had played the day before. When I arrived at the players' entrance, Frank Skaff, a Tiger scout, was waiting for me.

"We need you in Detroit, Hawk," he said. "Have you made any commitments?"

"Not yet."

"Well, don't without talking to Jimmy Campbell."

Campbell was the Tigers' general manager.

"O.K., Frank," I said. "I won't."

When I reached the locker room, Luke Appling called me into his office.

"Hawk, sit down," he said. "Now just relax. Charley didn't mean to fire you. You know how he is—he lost his head this morning. He wants you back. I want you back. We all want you back."

"If Charley wanted me back, he'd have called and asked me," I said. "And maybe I'd have gone back. But instead of calling me he called the commissioner's office and put me on the irrevocable waiver list."

"You can take yourself off," Appling said. "I'm sure Charley would make it worth your while."

"Luke," I said, "there's no way now that I'm coming back to play for this man. I don't care what he might offer me—I wouldn't take it."

"We've got a good ball club, Hawk. It's a great young club. It's not too many years away from a pennant. These guys are your friends. They love you and you love them."

"And I hate to leave them," I said. "But I will not play for Charley Finley."

Appling shrugged and said, "Well, if that's the way you feel, I .guess there isn't anything anyone can do."

We shook hands and I left. Appling was the wrong guy to ask me back. If Finley wouldn't do it himself, nobody could. And even Finley couldn't when I saw what he said about me in the afternoon newspapers. Asked why he hadn't sold me instead of releasing me, he replied, "After what Harrelson did to me, whatever I got for him would be blood money, and I don't take blood money."

Blood money? How ridiculous can you get?

The locker room was a madhouse of reporters, photographers, TV cameras, and announcers. They all crowded around, asking where I was going, when, and for how much. I didn't know any more than they did. All I knew was that the White Sox, the Tigers, the Twins, the Red Sox, and several other clubs had contacted me, and everybody was waiting for somebody else to make a move. Even while I was talking, one of the clubhouse men came over to tell me I had an important call.

It was Harry Dalton, the general manager of the Orioles. Had I decided anything? . . . How much did I want? . . . Would I play for the Orioles? . . . Would I talk to him before signing with anyone? . . .

After I hung up, Al Chapanis, the visiting-club locker-room man, came over and whispered, "Mr. Dark's been trying to get you all afternoon. He called here."

"Did you talk to him?" I said.

"No."

"Where is he?"

"I don't know."

"Al, you've got to find him," I said. "He's probably still in Washington."

I wanted to talk to Dark more than anyone. He had been around. He could read these front-office guys. He'd level with me, tell me who to sign with and for how much, help me make up my mind. If Al Chapanis could get hold of him before I saw Sully, I'd know what to say. All I had been doing was groping. I needed sound advice from somebody I could trust.

It took me an hour to get my bag packed while keeping the press happy. Just as I was about to go looking for Chapanis, he came over to tell me he had Alvin on the phone. Dark had checked into a little motel in Washington, and how the hell Al found him I'll never know. He must have gone right through the Washington phone book.

Dark and I talked a minute, then Alvin said, "Now, Hawk, you're in the best position of anyone in the whole history of baseball. As a free agent in the prime of your career, you'll collect a fortune. Before this thing is over, it could run up to a quarter of a million dollars, but I don't think you should let it."

"Why?" I said.

"Because you'll antagonize people. You can play one club against another just so far, but no farther. Don't short-change yourself, but don't be greedy. Anyway you look at it, you're going to get a lot of money. How many clubs have contacted you?"

"Most of the American League teams, I guess," I said. "I'm meeting Haywood Sullivan of the Red Sox at the airport in a little while."

"A nice guy and a fine organization," Alvin said. "They've got a good young ball club, with a chance to win the pennant. I'd like to see you with them."

"I still don't know what kind of money to ask," I said.

"See what they offer," Alvin said. "That will give you something to work on when you talk to the others."

After we made a date to fly back to Kansas City together the next day, I headed for the airport. When Sullivan and I were settled over a couple of drinks, he said, "What have you been offered?"

I wanted to say a hundred thousand dollars, but I couldn't. Nobody had offered me anything.

"Everybody wants to talk to me later," I said. "But I haven't had a concrete offer yet."

"How many clubs have you heard from?"

"Seven or eight—I don't know exactly."

"O.K.," Sully said. "We'll make you a firm offer right now."

He asked me how much I owed, how much salary I wanted, how much it cost to support my family, then came up with a package figure of something like eighty-eight thousand.

"You can't sign yet," he said. "But you can commit yourself right now and sign when the four days are up."

"No, I can't," I said. "I promised all the others I'd talk to them."

"Well, if you promised, you've got to talk to them. Get in touch with me in Boston as soon as you decide."

When I walked into my house in Kansas City late the next afternoon, Betty Ann said, "The phone hasn't stopped ringing all day. Call Mr. MacPhail. And Mr. Richards. They both said it was urgent."

Lee MacPhail was general manager of the New York Yankees, Paul Richards of the Atlanta Braves.

"I've never had so many urgent messages in my life," I said.

I decided to call Richards first. He's a close friend and one of my favorite golfing companions. Besides, Atlanta sounded interesting. I'm a Georgia boy, and I like the ball park there. The more I thought about it the better the idea seemed. I'd be practically home, in a town where I have a lot of friends, I could run down to Savannah whenever I felt like it. Atlanta sounded great.

A funny thing—now that I was away from all the excitement and hoopla about a quarter of a million bucks, I didn't think about it any more. Alvin was right. Maybe I could get that much, but I wasn't that hungry. All my life money had been important to me, but now that I had a chance to make a ton I didn't care. My needs are really pretty modest—a nice home for my family, settlement of my debts, good food, four or five thousand a year for clothes. I could be happy with a hundred thousand. Paul Richards would surely spring for that. And you can play golf in Atlanta practically all the year around, although I had sworn off for the baseball season.

I didn't reach Paul that night, but he called me the next day. We yakked back and forth, and he finally offered me a package deal of a hundred and twelve. That was all I wanted to hear, but I couldn't take it on the spot. I had to talk to all those other guys first. So this time I was the one who said I'd call back.

But my mind was practically made up. I'd go to Atlanta. All I had to do now was call people, thank them, tell them I was committed to another club, pack my golf clubs, and go. I couldn't play baseball for a couple of days. Richards and I would spend them on the golf course and then I'd join the Braves.

Except I had one little nagging doubt. The Red Sox were the most attractive team in baseball. Their owner, Tow Yawkey, was famous for his kindness and generosity to his ballplayers. Their general manager, Dick O'Connell, had done a fantastic job rebuilding them in only a couple of years. Their manager, Dick Williams, was tough, but a winner. They were in the heat of this pennant race and would be in the heat of plenty of others in the years to come. And Boston was a good town. But it was a long way from home, and Atlanta was so close. I could see my mother and Betty Ann could see her folks any time we wanted to.

I phoned Haywood Sullivan and said, "Sully, I got an offer I like and I think I'm going with this ball club."

"Don't commit yourself," he said. "We want you in Boston."

"Well, the offer's real good. Over a hundred thousand."

"Look, Hawk," Sullivan said. "Just because we made you one offer doesn't mean that we can't make you another. The figure doesn't scare us, and we want you here."

"I don't like to bargain, Sully," I said. "I suppose that's not good business, but I don't want to play one club against another. Besides, I really have made up my mind."

"Well—" Sullivan paused. Then he said, "Is it an American League club?"

I knew what that meant. The Red Sox were one of four clubs within two games of each other at the top of the American League standings. He didn't want me going to one of the other three.

"It's in the National League," I said.

"Well," he said, his voice relaxed, "that's fine, Hawk. I'm sorry we'll lose you, but if you've made up your mind, I guess there isn't much we can do."

That eliminated the last of my doubts about Atlanta, so I phoned Richards and accepted his offer.

"Fine," he said. "Come on down tomorrow and we'll hit a few golf balls."

I talked to so many people after that I can't remember all the conversations, or even the ractions. But a few stand out in my mind.

When, for example, I told Jimmy Campbell in Detroit that I had made up my mind, he said, "Isn't there anything we can do to change it?"

"I don't think so," I said.

"How much were you offered?"

"A hundred and twelve."

"That isn't that much money, Kenny," he said. "We want you here in Detroit. This is a good park for you. We've got a fine club with a good chance to win this year and in the years to come. What if I substantially topped the offer you got?"

I said, "Mr. Campbell, I'm happy with this ball club I'm going with. Really I am. Money isn't everything. When you get up that high, what difference does a few thousand make?"

And that was exactly the way I felt. I knew hundreds of guys who didn't have a hundred twelve thousand dollars. Who was I to stick my nose up at that kind of dough?

Then there was Harry Dalton in Baltimore. When I said I was going to get over a hundred thousand, he said, "Why, that's no money at all, Ken. You come on with us."

"Believe me, Mr. Dalton," I said, "I'm happy as can be with this ball club, and I know I'm going with them."

When I finally reached Calvin Griffith, we didn't talk about money at all. After a while he said, "If there isn't a chance of your coming with us, then I wish you luck. The main thing is going where you think you'll be happy."

I finished all the phone calls and was at peace with the world. I was going back to my home state, with my debts settled and money in the bank, and my future assured. I was getting the biggest salary of my life. My wife was happy to be near her folks and I was happy to be near mine.

That night Betty Ann and I were going over to Jack Haley's house for a few drinks and dinner, and then to the stadium to see the Kansas City Chiefs play the Chicago Bears—the first time the Chiefs ever played a National Football League club.

We were all dressed and ready to leave. I stood at a mirror to give myself one last admiring look. I had on a handsome gray suit, a white shirt, a bright-red necktie with a handkerchief to match, and alligator shoes. Thoroughly satisfied that I now looked every inch the big businessman, I joined Betty Ann at the front door— when the phone rang.

It was Dick O'Connell.

"Kenny," he said, "we've got to have you here in Boston."

"I'd love to go to Boston, Mr. O'Connell. But I have made a definite commitment to another club."

"You don't understand, Kenny. *We've got to have you here.* Haywood Sullivan tells me they offered you a hundred twelve."

"That's right," I said. "It seems an awful lot of money to me."

"How much will it take for us to get you up here?"

What the hell is the matter with me? I thought. *Since when am I so finicky about money? Here this guy is begging me to name my own figure to go to maybe the best organization in baseball in one of the best towns with a million opportunities to make money on the outside, and I'm playing hard-to-get. The hell with it.*

"A lot more than I'm getting," I said.

"Exactly how much?"

I took a deep breath and said, "A hundred fifty."

"You've got it," O'Connell said.

If I had said two hundred thousand he'd have said, "You've got it." Maybe he'd have said it if I had said a quarter of a million.

We talked for a few more minutes, then I called Paul Richards, thanking my stars that he was a good friend who wouldn't resent my backing out.

"Look, Paul," I said, "I just got an offer of a hundred fifty grand from Boston."

And Paul said, "Oh, gosh, Hawk—"

"I made a commitment to you," I said. "If you want me to keep it, I'll go down there without any hard feelings."

"Hawk, I know the shape you're in financially," Richards said. "I can't offer you that kind of money, and it's too much for you to turn down. You go ahead and take it."

"Sorry about the golf game," I said.

"We'll play some other time."

So the next day, instead of going to Atlanta to play golf with Paul Richards, I went to Boston to play baseball with the Red Sox.

15 | The Hawk Flies High

When I first joined the Red Sox in late August of 1967, I thought of the change only in technical baseball terms. I was leaving a last-place club for a potential winner. I was leaving first base, my regular position, for right field, where the Red Sox were hurting because they had just lost Tony Conigliaro for the season. And I was leaving a team where baseball interest had nearly been killed by Finley's continual threats to take it somewhere else for one backed not just by a city but by an entire section of the country.

For the Red Sox weren't just the Boston Red Sox. They were the New England Red Sox, with fans all the way from the Maritime Provinces of Canada to Hartford, Connecticut. And in 1967, when the Red Sox played at home, their devoted followers flocked to Fenway Park in packs. During the month of September, with the hottest pennant race in big-league history in progress, almost every game was a sellout.

I hadn't played before sellout crowds more than half a dozen times in my life. Now I played before them almost every day. I hadn't seen more than five or six newspapermen in a locker room ever since I broke into professional baseball. Now there were more writers and TV and radio people than players in the Red Sox locker room after every game.

HAWK

I could go into New York with the Athletics and hit two homers, and it would be worth maybe two little paragraphs in the Kansas City papers. I could drive in a run with an infield out for the Red Sox and my name was in national headlines. A winner in Boston made every man a hero. By the end of August, Kansas City didn't have any heroes. We had no pressure in Kansas City. We lived in a perpetual pressure cooker in Boston. Nothing anybody did in Kansas City meant much of anything. Everything everybody did in Boston meant something.

The day I reported to the Red Sox, there weren't two games separating the four top teams in the American League. Minnesota, Chicago, Detroit, and Boston were so close—and remained so close for the rest of the season—that any one of them might have won right up to the last week. The White Sox were eliminated a couple of days before the end, but each of the other three teams still had a chance on the last day of the season. Even after we beat the Twins in Boston that afternoon, we didn't clinch the pennant until the Tigers lost to the Angels in the second game of a double-header. If they had won, we would have had to meet them in a playoff to settle the race.

The pressure was fantastic—especially on me, who had rarely been sought out for interviews either in Kansas City or Washington. Now forty or fifty reporters milled around the locker room after every game, and even if I did nothing, someone always had something to ask me.

I felt the pressure and was pretty nervous all through that crazy, wonderful month of September, but I loved every minute of it. Guys react differently to pressure—some want to be left alone, others revel in it. I reveled. To be on a club in the thick of a pennant race, to have a chance to play in a World Series, to be the center of attention, to be interviewed every day by a writer or an announcer, or a dozen at a time, was all great.

For I am a ham at heart and hams love nothing more than the spotlight. At Kansas City there wasn't much spotlight for anyone. In Boston in 1967 the whole baseball world was just one gigantic spotlight.

It was the Year of the Yaz, as well it should have been. Yastrzemski performed miracles every day. He won the triple crown. He won the pennant for us. He made the impossible dream come true. He was in every way the Big Guy of the ball club. Without him, we might have finished fourth. Without him, we wouldn't have been in the race by September. It was Yaz's year, Yaz's pennant, Yaz's team, Yaz's thing. In 1967 this man was the greatest ballplayer who ever lived, in fact or in fiction. Compared to him, Frank Merriwell was a piker. Merriwell, the classic hero of sports fiction, hit in clutches only occasionally, made fantastic catches only in spots, ran to the right places, threw to the right bases, and made the right moves only here and there.

Yaz did all that almost every day. His reward was a bundle of money, a bundle of opportunities for making more money, a bundle of publicity, a bundle of national exposure on radio and television, a bundle of everything. And nobody begrudged him anything.

But a strange thing happened in Boston—the sort of thing I'm not sure might have happened anywhere else. With all his heroics and all the attention he got for them, Yaz didn't hog the whole spotlight. There was plenty of room in it for everybody on the ball club.

Including me. After all, I was a Johnny-come-lately to this almost legendary team. I came to it as an afterthought and through the luckiest of breaks. If Finley had fired me two weeks earlier, the Red Sox probably wouldn't have been interested in me, because they had no place to put me. Only Conigliaro's tragic accident, which nearly drove him out of the game for good, made it possible for the Red Sox to use me. They needed a long-hitting right-handed batter to play right field and follow Yaz in the batting order. I'm a long-hitting right-handed batter and can play right field. Charley Finley couldn't have found a better time to give me the ax. And I couldn't have found a better team or a better town to switch to.

For I'm not kidding myself—Boston made me. I had been the same mod, slightly mad character in Kansas City that I was in Boston. But the only real national exposure I got in Kansas City—or Washington either, for that matter—was as baseball's golf champion. In Kansas City I was Harrelson the journeyman first baseman who sometimes went on batting sprees, wore long hair and unconventional clothes, was one of the best golfers in the country outside the pro circuit, and caught everything that came his way with one hand even when he played in the outfield. The thing was, the only people who knew or gave a damn were in Kansas City. My foibles were meaningless because the foibles of a spotty hitter on a losing ball club in the heart of the Middle West are ignored. But the foibles of a slugger on a contending team in a big Eastern metropolitan center like Boston become an integral part of his charisma.

I didn't know what the hell charisma meant before I went to Boston. I didn't know I was supposed to have it until I lived there eight months. I thought living my life and doing my thing were of interest only to my family, my personal friends, and myself. In Boston, it was of interest to everybody. I was no longer Harrelson the journeyman first baseman who could play golf. I was the Hawk—everybody's Hawk. "Hawk" had been only a nickname before. Now it was a commodity.

Boston made it a commodity.

In Kansas City they weren't breaking down the doors to get me to appear as a guest speaker, or standing in line to get me to endorse products, or offering me all kinds of money-making deals, or stopping me in restaurants or movies or on the street for my autograph. I was well known in Kansas City, just as all big-league ballplayers are well known where they play, but nobody considered me a character anywhere else.

That's the big difference between playing in the Middle West and the East—specifically New York or Boston. New York, of course, is the big town for opportunities and nation-wide publicity, but Boston is a pretty good second. A star on a winning Red Sox team is known all up and down the East Coast to start with, and if he has a little something extra to offer he's soon a national figure. That rarely happens in the Middle West or the South. Outside of New York and Boston, the only town where a guy has a chance to make it big nationally is Los Angeles.

I didn't make it big nationally the minute I arrived in Boston. Despite the tremendous exposure that came under the circumstances of my going there, I began my Red Sox career on the bench. I hadn't played in eight days. The club was using various guys in right field—Jim Landis, George Thomas, and José Tartabull. With Landis in a Red Sox uniform less than a week and Thomas sort of a general handyman, Tartabull was the nearest thing to a regular right fielder the Red Sox had after Conigliaro was hurt.

Tartabull, a wonderful little guy who had been a teammate of mine with the Athletics, was at his best only in spots. Although a good fielder and one of the fastest men in the game, he was too small to hit the ball with much power and his throwing arm was weak. A left-handed spray hitter who came through with a surprising number of key hits, he didn't lose his job when I arrived. Manager Dick Williams platooned us the last month of the season, during which I didn't do a hell of a lot to distinguish myself.

To tell the truth, although I hit a home run off Bill Monbouquette in Yankee Stadium my first time up in a Red Sox uniform, I disappointed myself. I wanted so badly to help the club in that crazy pennant race that I tried too hard. Yet I did have my moments before the season was over.

In my twenty-one or twenty-two games with the Red Sox in the last weeks of the 1967 season, I drove in thirteen runs, almost all in big games. Against the White Sox one night, I came up with the bases loaded and cleaned them with a triple off Gary Peters. Later in the same game I drove in a run with a double and hit a home run.

And I won a game against Baltimore with a base hit off Eddie Watt. That was a big one, because, although the Orioles were out of the race by then, they were just murdering us in September. To beat them at that point was important to all of us. We were beginning to get a complex about Baltimore. We played the Orioles a lot in those last few weeks and they nearly knocked us right out of business.

Although I wish I could have done more to help, I was on cloud nine when we won that pennant. My whole big-league career had been spent with losers, and now, out of a clear sky, I was suddenly with a winner. I tell you, there is no thrill like playing in a World Series, especially when you never expect to get closer to one than a television set. Remember, I had started the season with Washington, which finished in a tie for sixth, then spent two and a half months with Kansas City, which finished last.

And now, as they began to play the national anthem before the first World Series game in Fenway Park, there I was out in right field in a Red Sox uniform. As I stood there with my cap in my hand, the tears actually rolled down my cheeks. I was crying like a baby when the game began.

I had a poor series, playing in four games, getting only one hit—a single—driving in only one run and batting .077. I can't tell you why I was so bad. All I know is that it was such a thrill to be with a winner that I never could imagine myself with a loser again.

Yet my future with the Red Sox was very doubtful. Nobody paid much attention to me until 1968 spring training, at which point everybody but the ball club traded me. I don't usually read the papers during the season, but that spring training I read them faithfully, just to see where the hell I was supposed to be going next.

"Harrelson's going to Detroit—Harrelson's going to Chicago—Harrelson's going to New York—" Day after day, some writer had me going somewhere, and day after day I thought surely I *was* going somewhere. Conigliaro was back with the club and, despite what eye doctors were saying about his being through, he did pretty well at the start of spring training. With him in right field and George Scott, who had hit .303 in 1967 on first base, what the hell could they do with me?

The trade stories didn't bother me. What did was that Manager Dick Williams paid no attention to me—hardly even spoke to me. This was his way, but I wanted to know where I stood. As it became obvious that Conigliaro wasn't going to make it back that year, if at all, I thought Williams would use me in right field. Instead, he had a rookie, Joe Lahoud, playing right in the exhibition games. When he announced he would give Lahoud every chance to make it, I went to see him at his office in Winter Haven.

"Richard," I said, "I'm not a ballplayer who's going to give you any trouble. I'm not one of those guys who will say, 'play me or trade me.' I was with you last year when you won a pennant. I love this ball club. I think we'll win it again and I want to stay with it. But I'm only twenty-six years old, and I want to play ball."

"Hawk," he said, "you're too good a ballplayer to sit on the bench. If we're not going to play you here, we'll trade you where you can play."

That was fair enough. He was telling it like it was. I walked out of his office satisfied that I'd be somebody's right fielder or first baseman. I hoped it would be Boston's. I loved the town, I loved the people, I loved the ball club, I loved everything. But if I had been traded at that time, I would have been satisfied. The Red Sox had given me a three-year contract under the terms that I signed with them. Whoever took me would have to pick up that contract, which called for a hefty salary through 1969.

One day when we played the Tigers in Winter Haven, one of their coaches came over to me and said, "Hawk, you'll be with us tomorrow. They're working on a deal right now."

"Fine," I said. "If I have to leave Boston, Detroit will be great."

But I didn't want to leave Boston. I was delighted the deal didn't go through—if there really was a deal in the works. It didn't even bother me to start the season on the bench. Lahoud had a great potential, but he was too young and inexperienced to make it in the majors. I kept myself in shape and sat back watching the kid in right field and Scott on first. The kid was in over his head. And Scotty, for no reason I could see, just fell apart at the plate. He seemed to have lost his touch completely.

Outside of a couple of pinch-hitting appearances, I didn't play for two weeks. All I did was keep in shape, pitch batting practice, and take plenty of it myself. I didn't hit a home run or drive in a run during the whole month of April. Williams didn't say a word to me, and I didn't go looking for him. I knew the Red Sox needed me, and I just sat back and waited.

One day Williams came over to my locker and said, "Hawk, get ready. I don't think the kid can do it."

"O.K.," I said.

The next day I was in right field. And right away I started hammering the hell out of the ball. I hit home runs, I drove in runs in bunches, I hit for average, I did it all. Scotty wasn't hitting, Yaz wasn't hitting, Conigliaro was on the sick list, and all of a sudden the Hawk was the big man on the ball club.

Wherever I went, writers, radio, TV people, photographers—a flock of characters representing every possible news medium—discovered something that had been there all the time. My hair was long, my clothes were sensationally different, I liked being where the action was, I was an egotist without being obnoxious about it, I spent money as fast as I got it—and sometimes faster—and, maybe more than anything else, I was a refreshing sort of guy in a sport which could always use refreshing sorts of guys. In other words, I was a character hitting like mad, leading the league in

RBIs, battling my old pal Hondo Howard for the home-run title, up among the first ten in the league in batting.

I was having the time of my life, both on and off the field. And learning—learning new things about baseball and about myself simply through the things that happened almost every day. I talked more baseball than I ever had before, and with more people who knew more than I did. Baseball is a complicated game, far more complicated than fans realize. And it's a wonderful fun game. I had always enjoyed it, but never as much as in 1968, when Harrelson the journeyman really became Hawk the character.

People asked me things about myself nobody had asked me before. They were noticing me. I liked that. I want to be noticed. I want people to be curious about me. I want them to ask for my autograph. The day they stop, the day Hawk the character becomes Harrelson the journeyman, the day I can't laugh at myself, the day the action ends will be the saddest day of my life.

That's why I'll never forget 1968. The only bad thing about it was that we didn't win the pennant. But it was a year of wonderful action for me, a year full of odd little incidents that will always be with me.

Like the time in Yankee Stadium on a humid, lazy sort of night, with maybe eight thousand people rattling around in that huge ball park. When I trotted out to right field in the Yanks' half of the first inning, I heard a familiar, "Hey, Hawk, howya doing?"

I looked up, and there was Bill Mathis of the Jets sitting with a couple of good-looking girls. Mathis is a buddy of Joe Namath's, and I've spent many a happy hour in Joe's famous Manhattan pad with Bill, whom everyone calls Birdman.

"Hey, Birdman," I yelled, "what's happening?"

"Not much," he said. "You're having a pretty good year, aren't you?"

"Yeah, not bad. When are you guys starting?"

"Next week," Mathis said.

"What kind of a club you going to have?" I yelled.

"Hell of a club," he said. "We're going all the way."

Every inning we yelled back and forth. In the meantime, I was having a rough night—struck out twice, I think—and along about the seventh inning of a tie game Mathis yelled, "Hey, Hawk, hit one in the stands. I'm sick of seeing you strike out every time."

"O.K.," I said, "you've got it. Next time I'll hit the first pitch out of here."

The next time I came up, Joe Verbanic, the Yankee pitcher, tried to slip a fast ball by me. I must have hit that thing nine miles. When I ran out to right field after the inning was over, there was Mathis kneeling on his seat salaaming while the girls grinned and waved.

Like the night with Sandy Koufax, whom I used to see whenever we were on nationwide TV. We were in Boston—I guess it was in early August when I was murdering the ball. Sandy, who was working the next day's game with the NBC-TV crew, came over and said, "So the Hawk is for real, huh?"

I said, "Hell, yes, big guy."

After a little kidding back and forth, I said, "Sandy, you staying at the Somerset?"

"Yes."

"Come up to the room for a couple of drinks after the game."

Denny McLain, with twenty-four wins already, was pitching against us for the Tigers that night. Before the game, I said, "Denny, if you win thirty this year are you going for a hundred grand?"

"I'm going for it," he said. "If I win thirty I'll have it coming to me."

"I hope to hell you get it," I said.

Well, that night he beat us for his twenty-fifth win of the season. The one chance we had to get him he loaded the bases with nobody out and Dalton Jones, Yaz, and me coming up. Everybody in the ball park knew if we didn't break the game wide open then we never would.

Well, McLain just blew Jones away with three fast balls, and he got Yaz with three more, and I went up there with my adrenalin running, ready to hit that damn fast ball right into Kenmore Square. Maybe he could get Dalton and Yaz with those things, but he wasn't going to get me. I could see that ball disappearing over the left-field screen and me running around the bases with those three guys waiting at the plate for me and thirty thousand fans going crazy and the whole Red Sox dugout coming out to greet me.

I was all set for the fast ball, and McLain fed me a slider on the outside corner of the plate. I knew it was a strike, but couldn't even swing at it.

Well, I thought, *he won't do that again—not the way his fast ball is exploding.*

So I stood there ready for the fast ball, and McLain came in with another slider in exactly the same spot. There wasn't a thing I could do but watch it go by. I was so handcuffed I couldn't have hit it with a snowshoe.

He won't throw me three of them, I thought. *He'll pour on that fast ball for sure this time.*

Now I was set for the fast ball again, and what do you suppose McLain did? You guessed it—he threw me another slider, and I was out of there on three pitches without taking the bat off my shoulder.

He struck me out another time that night. My last time up—in the eighth inning with the Tigers leading us by seven or eight runs—I got into the batter's box, looked out at Denny, and yelled, "You sonofagun, you ought to get a hundred and fifty grand next year."

He and Bill Freehan, the catcher, laughed so hard they had to hold up the game.

HAWK

Up in my room at the Somerset after the game Koufax and another guy—I think it was Chet Simmons, the producer of the TV show—were sipping drinks with me when Sandy said, "I've seen a lot of baseball games. I've seen a lot of pitchers and a lot of pitches. And I want to tell you those were three of the greatest pitches I've ever seen one pitcher throw to a hitter in a situation like that. He had struck out two good hitters with fast balls they couldn't see. You *had* to go up there looking for the same thing. And he gave you three perfect sliders that nobody in the world set for a fast ball could have hit."

Like the time we played Cleveland at Fenway Park, with Luis Tiant pitching for the Indians. The game was on national TV, when I was always at my worst. The last time I had faced Tiant I struck out, then hit three homers, two off him, and batted in all the runs in a 7–0 Red Sox win.

Tiant's a Cuban who can't pronounce "Hawk." He calls me "Honk." A great pitcher and a great guy whom everybody likes. While I was in the batting cage, he walked by and said, "Honk, I'm going to blow your ass away four times today."

"What are you talking about, Louie?" I said. "Get out of here, man. Go over there and sit in the dugout. Last time I saw you I jacked you for two homers."

"Four times, Honk. You watch."

First time up, with my mama watching in Savannah and my friends watching all over the country, he threw three fast balls right by me. He struck me out again the second time up, then fanned me again my third time. The Indians were leading us by six, seven runs when I got up the fourth time.

I put three fingers up and yelled, "Luis, three times all right, but not four—not on national TV."

He threw one right down the pipe. I was so anxious I topped it, and it rolled out to the shortstop. And when I looked at Tiant he was grinning and holding up four fingers and yelling, "See, Honk? See, Honk? See, Honk?"

I saw. So did my mama in Savannah and my friends all around the country.

Like the time we were playing the Tigers and we pulled up even with them after they had an eight-run lead. This was a national-TV game, too. They scored a run in the ninth to go ahead, then I came up with two out and nobody on. Don McMahon was pitching, and I knew he was going to throw me nothing but junk. When the count went to three balls and no strikes, I got the sign from Eddie Popowski, our third base coach, to hit away if I liked the pitch.

I figured he'd throw one low and away to walk me. That was just where it came, and I golfed it into the screen for a home run to tie it up. Freehan, who finally beat us with a homer in the tenth, asked me the next day, "How in the hell did you hit that pitch? It was six inches off the ground and six inches outside."

"I was looking for it, Bill," I said.

"I've heard of guys looking for low outside pitches," he said. "But I never saw anybody hit one over the fence that low and that far outside."

Like psyching myself in Detroit right after I hit those three homers in one game in Cleveland. Joe Sparma was pitching for the Tigers, and he always gave me trouble. We still had a shot at the pennant—we were maybe four or five games behind the Tigers— and I sat in front of my locker before the game, psyching.

I wouldn't talk to anyone—just sat there with my eyes closed, visualizing Sparma throwing the ball, visualizing me hitting it. I could see his sinker coming, and his slider, and his good curve ball, and I could see myself lining the ball over short, hitting one into the stands. By the time the game started, it was all up there in my mind, the way I was going to get Sparma.

He struck me out the first time, made me pop up the second,

made me ground out the third, and all my visions were going to hell. I came up in the eighth with guys on second and third, two out, and the Tigers leading, 3–2. I knew Sparma wouldn't give me anything really good to hit, but he didn't want to walk me because Reggie Smith followed me and Smith always hit him better than I did.

I psyched myself right up to the last minute—closed my eyes and saw Sparma pitching me a fast ball down but in the strike zone. I swung at the first pitch and missed it, swung at the second and missed that, and now Sparma had me 0 and 2. The next three were close, but I laid off all of them, and the count was 3 and 2. I stepped out of the batter's box and thought, *It'll be a fast ball down. He'll throw it because he always gets me on it.* And I closed my eyes and saw that ball coming and saw myself hitting it right into kingdom come.

Back in the batter's box, I watched Sparma take his stretch, come down to the belt, then throw his pitch. Before it left his arm, I was saying over and over, "Stay back, Hawk, stay back, stay back." And I knew it was coming down and away and that I had to stay back until the very last minute, then come around fast.

I saw Sparma let the ball go and I saw its flight and I saw it coming just where I had visualized it—down and away. I held back until that last split second, then swung and hit the ball as squarely as I've ever hit one in my life. And that time everything happened the way it was supposed to happen. The ball went off my bat like a shot, and soared high toward left center field.

I didn't have to close my eyes to see the rest of my vision. It was right there in front of me, a home run from the instant it left the bat, so obviously a home run that for a second or two I stood at the plate and watched it. It landed in the lower deck of the stands, and won us a 5–3 victory.

When I went to the outfield, some crazy kooks bombarded me with firecrackers. I got hit in the back with a fire bomb and they had to stop the game, but I didn't care. My adrenalin was still running so fast that I didn't feel any pain until I got back into the locker room.

Like how I figured the Athletics might have won the pennant if they had kept me. In Oakland by then, they finished sixteen or seventeen games out. If they had my thirty-five home runs and my hundred and nine RBIs, they might have won the pennant. Yes, I mean the pennant, man.

Hell, in one stretch that summer I hit twenty homers that put the Red Sox ahead when they were either tied or behind, and four more that tied games. Only six of the thirty-five I hit in the season came with the teams more than two runs apart. I won twelve games with homers alone, which broke a Red Sox record of ten held by Ted Williams. And that didn't count other games I won with lesser hits.

Put me in that Oakland lineup and I'd have won at least twelve games. Those guys were only eleven games out by Labor Day. They had a great young team, but couldn't score runs. If Charley Finley hadn't given me away, I might have won them the pennant in that Oakland park. As Alvin Dark had warned, I let that Kansas City ball park lick me, but the Oakland park wouldn't have. I hit five homers there as a visiting ballplayer. I'd have hit fifteen or twenty in an Athletics uniform.

I hit seven homers altogether against the Athletics in 1968, batted about .400, drove in eighteen runs against them. They beat us more than we beat them, as it was—ten games to our eight—and I won six of those eight myself. So there were six more games they might have won with me on their side.

Finley fired Alvin Dark, the best manager in baseball, in 1967. Finley fired me in 1967, when I was swinging a hot bat, and he didn't have me in 1968 when I was hotter. Finley fired his new manager, Bob Kennedy, after Kennedy had done a great job in 1968. Finley is always firing key men, and that's why he doesn't win pennants. Dark would have won him a pennant. Given a chance, Hank Bauer, who replaced Kennedy as manager in 1969, can win him a pennant. But I don't think anybody's going to win Charley Finley a pennant until he keeps his hands off his ball club and lets baseball men run it.

So much for Finley. So much for what happened to me on the field in 1968. Look what happened to me off it.

Hitting the way I was hitting, I had the world by the ears. Offers came pouring in—for business opportunities, for television shows, for appearances here, there, and everywhere. They weren't little offers, small-money offers, hundred-buck offers like what I used to get in Washington and Kansas City, but big offers, four- and five-figure offers. In Kansas City I had to duck guys trying to collect what I owed them. In Boston I had to take my telephone receiver off the hook to duck the guys trying to dump money into my lap.

The mod man with the long hair and the crazy clothes was in such demand he couldn't walk across his hotel lobby or along the street or into the ball park without someone coming up with a sure-fire proposition that was going to make him an instant millionaire.

Nothing like that had ever happened to me before. I never needed anyone to take care of my financial affairs in Kansas City. The only financial affairs I had were debts I couldn't pay except by winning on the golf course or at the pool table or in gin rummy, the only card game I play much.

Now I had to have some expert help. I couldn't tell the difference between a legitimate deal and a phony one. I didn't know who was on the level and who was trying to take advantage of me. How the hell did I know what to sign and what to lay off?

I finally went to Carl Yastrzemski. He was the only guy on the Red Sox who had been through anything like this.

"Look," I said, "I drink Yaz milk. I eat Yaz bread. I read Yaz's book. I try to concentrate like Yaz, to hit like Yaz, to do things Yaz's way. Now I need Yaz's advice. For crissake, what do I do about all those offers I'm getting?"

"Call Bob Woolf," he said.

"Who's Bob Woolf?"

"He's a lawyer," Yaz said. "He handles the finances for a lot of athletes—most of the Celtics and the Bruins and the Patriots, and plenty of guys in other towns. He knows athletes. He knows their needs and how to get the most out of their dough. He runs a big law office, and athletes are his favorite people. He'll show you how to handle your problems as soon as he knows what they are."

So I called Bob Woolf—Robert G. Woolf, attorney-at-law. A Jewish boy who went through Boston College, a Catholic institution, on a basketball scholarship. Young, loves sports, loves athletes—a real fan, with a brain like a steel trap.

Signing up with Bob Woolf was the smartest thing I ever did in my life. You wouldn't believe the mess my finances were in. I had just bought a fifty-thousand-dollar home in Lynnfield, where Yaz lives. I didn't know how much money I had, how much I had spent, how close I was to being broke again—nothing.

After looking over my affairs, Bob said, "Don't worry. I'll take care of everything, but you'll have to let me make the decisions. The first one is that from now on you're on an allowance. Everything else goes into investments of some kind."

"What if I overdraw on my allowance?" I said.

"You won't," Bob said.

He really didn't mean that. I know. As I write these lines a year later, I'm about fourteen-thousand-dollars overdrawn. But I've made so much it doesn't matter. Bob keeps after me to keep within the allowance, but I know he has told others that my overdrawing only fourteen Gs was better than he expected.

I have to ask him every so often what deals I'm in. I own substantial stock in things I never heard of, thanks largely to Murray Shear, president of the Industrial Bank and Trust of Everett, of which I am now a stockholder. I have a piece of the Washington Planning Corporation, a diversified investment outfit. A guy named Bill Coltin, its president, is one of my favorite golf fish. No matter

221

how big a handicap I give him, I always beat him. I'm in Gemini Films, Inc., and in the Brandywine TV Producing Company. I've got an interest in the Geisha Steak House, a new Japanese restaurant in Boston. I own part of Indian Meadow, a golf club in Westboro, Massachusetts.

John Thomas (not the high jumper) and I own Santoro's, a sandwich place in Lynn. We're planning to open a flock of others like it and call them the Hawk shops. We're planning a night spot called the Hawk's Nest, and a clothing store called Harrelson's of Boston. Shear and Woolf, among others, will be in some or all of these enterprises.

Woolf encourages me to do my thing—hit the ball and be Hawk the character. That's easy. I was doing it anyhow. Besides hair and clothes that are distinctively me, practically everything I touch is distinctively me. My dune buggy is the damnedest thing you ever saw, and my pad in Brookline looks like Joe Namath moved there from New York. The dune buggy was built especially for me.

Namath would love my pad. Half the living room is a bar, complete with mirrors, making the room look twice its size. The walls are orange, the ceiling black, the rugs white. Nothing but pillows and a hi-fi in the living room except for the bar. There's a big hawk clutching a rat on the counter, and a multicolored fountain in back.

There's almost nothing in the bedroom but a white rug and a huge round bed with a leopard-skin blanket and an orange spread. I use a smaller bedroom for a dressing room, with clothes all over the place, and shoes stacked in a big bookcase.

The tiling in the bathroom and the kitchen has either the word "Hawk" or pictures of hawks as part of the decor. There are so many hawks all over the place that it couldn't be anyone else's but mine. Nobody else could live in it. (I wonder if anyone else would want to.)

I had a ball through the winter of 1968–69. As the American

League player-of-the-year and the league's RBI leader, I was showered with attention wherever I went. The city of Savannah had a wonderful Hawk Harrelson day, with honors for my mama, parades and golf and parties and all sorts of other things. I was a nominee for the Academy of Professional Sports in Hollywood, I had that TV show and was featured in that rock number, "Don't Walk the Hawk." I had so many offers that even Bob Woolf went nuts sorting them out. A German baron invited me into the Knights of Malta, and somebody sent an "urgent" wire inviting me to make a movie.

Man, I was living! When I got to Winter Haven for 1969 spring training, I figured I was home free. Even when Tony Conigliaro made a miraculous comeback after a year's layoff and got his right-field job back, I figured I was home free. The Red Sox, having lost Joe Foy to the new expansion club in Kansas City, shifted George Scott from first base to third and put me on first. All that trade talk I had heard the year before stopped. Who the hell would dream of trading the Hawk now?

I was riding high when we got home to Boston for the start of the championship season. I had a regular job at a hell of a salary. Boston and I had a wild love affair going. The town was mine and I was its boy. I had dozens of things going for me, with new ones coming along all the time. I had my dune buggy, my pad, my businesses, everything. I could go down to Lynnfield to see my kids whenever I wanted to. Betty Ann still was mad at me, but except for that, life was good—perfect, in fact. I was richer, happier, busier than I had ever been. All I had to do to keep things that way was stay in Boston. I didn't consider the possibility of leaving. After the year I had had in 1968, why should the Red Sox deal me off?

Why indeed?

On Saturday, April 19, the game between the Red Sox and the

HAWK

Indians was called off on account of rain. At about one-thirty in the afternoon, Alvin Dark, now managing the Indians, phoned. He was all excited, happy as could be.

"Welcome, Hawk," he said. "Boy, am I glad to have you!"

I thought he was crazy. "What are you talking about?" I said.

"You mean you didn't know?"

"Didn't know what?"

"You're with us now," Alvin said. "The Red Sox just traded you to Cleveland."

16 | Lost Weekend Regained

For maybe ten seconds I sat in front of my bar, the telephone in my hand, my mind a blank, my throat so tight I couldn't say a word. I felt as if something hard and heavy had hit me in the pit of the stomach, or as if someone in the family had died.

I couldn't make sense, couldn't gather my thoughts, couldn't do anything but sit there like a dope. Finally I said, "Alvin—please—let me talk to you later."

After I hung up, I called Dick O'Connell. "Is it true?"

"Yes, Hawk," he said. "It's true. I tried to call you but your line was busy."

"Alvin just told me."

"Well, as long as it was somebody on our club or theirs," O'Connell said. "I just didn't want you hearing it from an outsider or on the air or something. We're not releasing it until later in the day."

"What was the deal?"

"You, Ellsworth, and Pizarro for Siebert, Azcue, and Romo."

"Can I see you, Dick?"

"Come on down," he said.

Shook as I was driving to Fenway Park in the dune buggy, I realized it looked like a good deal for the Red Sox. Sonny Siebert was

225

an experienced right-handed pitcher, Joe Azcue a solid catcher, Vincente Romo one of the best short relief men in the league. Dick Ellsworth, who had had a good year for us in 1968, was a lefty, and Fenway Park kills southpaws. Juan Pizarro was a journeyman reliefer who had been all over both leagues.

And me. What the hell was I? American League player-of-the year? What did that mean to the Red Sox? They were loaded with batting power—Yaz, Conigliaro, Andrews, Jones, Petrocelli, Smith, Scott maybe coming back.

But how could they trade me? The most popular guy on the team. The most colorful guy in baseball. When hot, the best hitter in the business. And now I was gone.

Man, I mean gone. I didn't know what the hell to do. I couldn't go to Cleveland. Everything I had, everything going for me, everything that meant anything to me except my mama was right here in Boston. How could I leave?

In a daze, I walked up to O'Connell's office after parking the buggy in the player's lot at Fenway Park. What could I say? What could he say? Where did we stand? What was I doing there anyhow?

As we shook hands, Dick said, "Hawk, I'm truly sorry. This wasn't a deal we wanted to make—we *had* to make it."

"I know it was a good deal for us," I said.

Why do I say "us"? I thought. *"Us" is Cleveland—if I go there. My God, do I have to?*

". . . Pizarro's out on waivers," O'Connell was saying. "We lose him anyhow. With Lonborg doubtful, we've got to have a starting right-hander like Siebert. We couldn't get along with the catching we had. Azcue fills that spot."

"I know—I know," I said.

Why me? I thought.

"They needed hitting. We needed pitching—"

I guess I was with Dick half an hour, then went to the locker room and stretched out disconsolately on a trunk, my velvet trousers, my white boots, my Edwardian haircut being shot at from all angles by still photographers and TV guys. There were Cleveland and Boston wire-service writers around, and people kept asking me what I was going to do.

Yaz came over and said, "Is it true?"

I nodded.

"Where are you going now?" Yaz said.

"Back to my pad," I said. "Come up. Cheez—I don't want to be alone. And I have to make some phone calls."

I got hold of Bill Coltin and asked him to go to the apartment. But the guy I wanted most to talk to was Bobby Woolf, and he was in Phoenix, negotiating Neal Walk's contract with the basketball Suns there. Walk was second to Lew Alcindor in the pro draft and had engaged Bobby as his attorney. Bobby had left only that morning. I didn't know if he had arrived in Arizona yet.

I wanted my kids. We had just had a fourth one, and Betty Ann couldn't drive them in. I got hold of John Thomas, who said he'd bring the three older ones in for the night. And I wanted to talk to Mike Andrews. He was my best friend on the ball club. I tried to get him, but there was no answer at his house. He lived in Peabody, near Lynnfield.

Still so shook I hardly knew what I was doing, I drove back to the pad. Yaz and Lahoud followed me. Coltin was already there. Wendell, my houseboy, was pacing back and forth, tears running down his cheeks. There was a message that the kids were on the way in with Thomas.

I went into the bedroom and reached Woolf at his hotel in Arizona.

"Bobby," I said, "you're not going to believe this, but I was traded."

There was a long silence—ten seconds, maybe. Then Woolf said, "You're kidding. They wouldn't trade you."

"They did. Bobby, I need help. Can you come back?"

"I just got here," he said. "I won't be but a few hours, and then I'll take the first plane east I can get."

"Bobby—" I was almost crying—"I think I'm going to quit. I can't believe this is happening. I'm just hurt so badly. Tell me—can I afford to quit?"

"I don't know, Hawk. I've got to think about it. We'll go over everything in the morning."

"Bobby, I want to quit. Can you fix up a press conference for tomorrow?"

"Let's think about it," he said. "Wait until I get back."

"I want a press conference tomorrow," I said. "I'm not going to play in Cleveland."

"O.K.," he said. "Even if you don't quit, a press conference won't hurt, I suppose. But you've got to sleep on this."

John Thomas came in with the three older children—Patricia, Mike, and Ricky. The kids kissed me, and I told them they could all sleep in the round bed. It's so big that even with a grownup in it, kids can sleep around the edges.

I paced back and forth, talking to Yaz, talking to Coltin, talking to Thomas. Wendell kept asking what I wanted, then made sandwiches for everybody. Barry Price and Gerry Fineberg, who owned the building and were in on some of our enterprises, dropped by, and all afternoon and evening we were going from my apartment to Barry's to Gerry's and back to mine.

Yaz was almost as shook as I was.

"I've got to quit," I told him. "I can't leave Boston."

"Make sure you can before you do," Yaz said.

"What would you do?"

"I don't know," he said. "I just don't know. I'm older than you and I've been around longer and practically everything I have is here. I guess I'd quit, too, rather than leave Boston. I don't know—"

Lenny Shapiro, one of the lawyers in Bobby's office phoned and said we'd have a press conference there at twelve-thirty Sunday, the next day. I'd announce my retirement—I couldn't do anything else.

The afternoon papers had me all over the front page. HAWK TRADED—the screaming headline dwarfed Vietnam, Presidential statements, campus unrest, race problems—everything. Fans were quoted and columnists pontificated and everybody seemed to have the same opinion. *How could the Red Sox trade the Hawk?*

One quote stuck in my mind. Hot Rod Hundley of the Cubs said, "I can't understand the Red Sox trading Harrelson. It's like the Celtics trading Bob Cousy for Paul Revere. Not even in the same century, man."

Today I can laugh about it. When I first saw it, I couldn't even smile.

Boston writers kept calling, asking what I was going to do. The conversations all were practically the same.

"Are you going to Cleveland?"

"I don't know."

"Will you retire?"

"I don't know."

After Shapiro announced the press conference, I just kept referring people to that. I'd make the announcement then. But I had to talk to Bobby Woolf and Bobby Woolf was in Arizona.

As the night wore on, my nerves became more frayed. I couldn't sleep, couldn't eat, couldn't stand up, couldn't sit down, couldn't do anything. Yaz and Lahoud left for home around seven or eight, I guess. I tried Mike Andrews, and a babysitter answered. He and his wife were out and weren't expected back until about eleven. I wanted Mike—just had to talk to him. I called him again at eleven and talked to Marilyn, his wife. He was driving the sitter home.

"He'll go right in when I tell him you called," she said. "He can spend the night there."

Mike showed up around midnight. By then I was alone with the kids. The two older ones, Patricia and Mike, were asleep, but Ricky, the little one, had been restless and I had him on my lap in back of the bar. With Ricky dozing in my arms, Andrews and I talked a couple of hours. He didn't want me to retire, thought it was a mistake—but I was sure I'd quit. But I couldn't make up my mind until Woolf arrived.

I didn't know it then, but Bobby was on a puddle-jumping flight that had left Phoenix at ten o'clock, one a.m. Boston time. It stopped at every way station across the country, and Bobby didn't get a wink of sleep. By the time he arrived in Boston—at about nine in the morning—he was exhausted.

So was I. Andrews, who had a ball game to play Sunday afternoon, went to sleep on the pillows and cushions in the living room. I finally got little Ricky quieted down and to sleep on the big bed, but I couldn't sleep myself. I paced most of the night, maybe dozing a little, but too keyed up to get any real rest.

Barry Price, Gerry Fineberg, and Lee Walls—he's a former big-league ballplayer now living in Boston and associated with several of the enterprises I was in—came over in the morning. Bobby Woolf arrived at about ten. He had already talked to the others, and they had agreed that I could afford to quit baseball if I insisted —that the Washington Planning Corporation could guarantee my baseball salary for three years in case I gave it up.

The apartment was a madhouse—Wendell fixing things to eat and watching the kids, Mike Andrews half-asleep on the living-room floor, Bill Coltin pacing around, Gerry and Barry and Lee talking about what I ought to do, me pacing, Woolf, his eyes red from lack of sleep, trying to get organized.

The one thing that stands out in my mind was Andrews waking up, looking at Woolf, and saying, "Did you fly all night?" When Bobby said he had, Mike got up, went to the bar, and said, "I'll fix you breakfast—a nice Bloody Mary."

And Woolf said, "Leave out the vodka." He doesn't drink.

Bobby and I went into the bedroom and Bobby said, "O.K., we've got it doped out. I don't advise it"—he was looking hard at me—"because I think you'd be crazy to retire, but you can afford to. I hope you've changed your mind about it."

"Well, I haven't," I said. "I'm quitting. Why shouldn't I? My heart's in Boston, my business interests are here, everything that means anything is here. I can't leave."

"And you can't quit playing ball either," Woolf said. "Even though you can afford it, you'll be an emotional wreck if you quit now. Why, it's only April. There's a whole season to go. You can't sit through it without going nuts."

"Bobby, I'm going to retire. If I can't play for the Red Sox I don't want to play for anyone."

Bobby shrugged and said, "O.K., Hawk. If that's the way you feel. Just be sure, that's all."

It was around eleven now, and I said, "Let's go to the ball park."

I put on a maize sweater, multicolored slacks, white high-heeled boots, and dark glasses, and we drove to Fenway Park in Bobby's car, ignoring his mobile phone, which rang steadily. The ball park was already mobbed. People were picketing in the streets, carrying signs like, THE HELL WITH THE RED SOX. WE WANT THE HAWK, and WE LOVE YOU, HAWK, and NEVER MIND THE PENNANT. LET'S HAVE THE HAWK, and DON'T LEAVE US, HAWK. It choked me up pretty good, believe me.

In the Red Sox locker room, players crowded around asking, "What's happening? What's happening?"—and I couldn't tell them. All I did was shrug and tell them we'd make an announcement soon. Manager Dick Williams pulled us aside and said, "What are you going to do, Hawk?"

"I'm going to retire," I said. "I'm just going to give it up. Too many other interests in Boston, I've got to stay here."

Dick shook his head, obviously more perplexed than sore.

231

"Gee," he said, "I don't know what's going to happen now." He shook hands, wished me luck, and then went into his office.

Then we walked under the stands to the visiting locker room to see Alvin. The Cleveland players were great—they crowded around to shake hands and tell me how glad they were I was with them, and all that. When we reached Alvin's office, he said, "Man, am I glad to see you! You can mean a pennant for us."

"Alvin," I said, "you're my best friend in baseball. I'd rather play for you than anyone. But I've got to explain this to you personally. I don't want you to get it from anyone else. I'm going to retire."

He stared, and said, "Retire? At twenty-seven? With your best years ahead of you? Hawk, are you out of your mind?"

"No, I can afford to retire," I said. "Here—Bobby will tell you."

When Woolf had explained all the things I had going for me in Boston, Alvin said, "Hawk, I never realized this because I've never seen anything like it before. It never happened to me or to any other ballplayer I've ever heard of. I hate to see it happen, but I guess you could retire if you wanted to."

It was after twelve, and we had to hurry to reach the press conference. Later, I heard that Alvin phoned his boss, Gabe Paul, the president of the Indians, who was in Tampa, and Paul said he'd meet the team the next day in Baltimore.

We drove to Woolf's office in Allston, about two miles from the ball park. When we arrived, we were astonished to see the crowd. Hundreds of people were milling around there, yelling for me, holding up signs telling me how much they loved me. Bobby had to park in the middle of the street, and we went upstairs, where we had to fight our way through cameras and all the other equipment of the news media. There must have been a hundred writers there, guys from all over the place.

Before we sat down in Bobby's private office, he murmured, "Are you sure you want to do this?"

"Positive," I said.

"I know you can economically," he said. "But emotionally?"

"Bobby, I'm through. Tell them I'm through."

After Woolf made the formal announcement of my retirement, he explained all my enterprises, the agreement that my salary would be guaranteed for three years, the absolute necessity of my staying in Boston. Then I said I didn't blame anyone, that this was part of baseball, that I still loved the Red Sox, that I loved the Indians, that I wasn't bitter or anything, but that I just couldn't leave Boston.

Then someone asked Woolf, "Would the Hawk go to Cleveland if the Indians made up his losses in leaving Boston?"

"I don't know," Bobby said.

"That's not why I'm retiring," I said. "I'm not looking for anything from Cleveland, and I don't expect to get anything from Cleveland. I have to play in Boston or I can't play anywhere."

"What happens to the deal?"

"I don't know," I said.

I was worried, unhappy, scared, hurt. I really didn't know what would happen to the deal. As soon as my retirement announcement came out, the Indians and the Red Sox agreed to freeze all the players involved until the situation was resolved. That meant five other guys—Siebert, Romo, Azcue, Ellsworth, and Pizarro—couldn't play, even though all were in their new uniforms.

To complicate matters, Siebert and Azcue had both already announced they would not go back to the Indians, no matter what happened. It was a loused-up mess—and the only one who could unravel it was me. Even as the press conference broke up, Bobby said, "The pressure is all going to be on you, Hawk. You'll be blamed for everything. People are with you now. They know how hurt you are. But they can change overnight—and so can you."

"I won't change," I said. Then, "Come on, Bobby, let's go to the ball game."

We went up to see O'Connell in his office at Fenway Park. He

233

was pretty shook himself when we told him I was through. So was Haywood Sullivan. Bobby said he hoped things could get straightened out, and I agreed. But I still insisted I couldn't play for anyone but the Red Sox. And O'Connell insisted there was no way—no way at all—that they could take me back.

We watched an inning or two from a roof box, but I couldn't sit still. I saw myself out on the field with the "40" on my back, and went crazy. Bobby was watching me closely, and when I said, "I've never seen a game from up here," he said, "Hawk, this isn't doing you a bit of good. You shouldn't be watching. Not now."

He drove me back to my apartment, then left. Bill Coltin, Gerry Fineberg, and Barry Price were there with Wendell and the kids. They had the Bruins-Canadiens Stanley Cup hockey game on television in the bedroom. Normally, I'm a wild hockey fan, but when I lay down to watch I could hardly keep my eyes open. Even when my pal Derek Sanderson, another of Woolf's clients, scored for the Bruins, I couldn't get excited. The night was a horror, just as the previous night had been. The kids stayed with me, and people kept coming in and out.

At eleven—this was Sunday night—Bobby phoned.

"Gabe Paul called," he said. "He said he'd be in touch with us tomorrow."

I didn't sleep much. Just paced most of the night. By Monday morning, I had had a few catnaps, but was utterly exhausted. At ten, Bill Coltin came by.

"Come on out to Indian Meadow," he said. "A round of golf will relax you."

So we drove to the golf course—about thirty miles from Boston —where we ran into Dr. Pat DiCicco, who often played with us. When we went to the locker room to change our clothes, I suddenly stopped and said, "Gee, Bill, I can't play golf. It will louse up my baseball swing."

"I thought you were giving up baseball," Bill said.

234

"They're two different swings," I said.

"So you're not going to retire."

"I didn't say that."

"How about a putting match?" Bill said. "Would that hurt your baseball swing?"

We went to the putting green with Dr. DiCicco, and I gave them each a stroke a hole. They murdered me. I couldn't sink a putt— didn't care whether I did or not. My mind just wasn't on it.

After lunch, we went to Santoro's in Lynn—the submarine place John Thomas and I own. John had driven the kids home and met me there. I put on an apron and served sandwiches and signed autographs and kept telling people I was through—that the Red Sox were my team and if I couldn't play for them I wouldn't play for anybody. They cheered and mobbed me, and I felt a little better, but not much.

At four in the afternoon, I had a call from Gabe Paul.

"Will you come to New York tonight and meet me at '21' for dinner?" he said.

"How did you know I was here?" I said.

"Bob Woolf told me."

"Will you check back in fifteen minutes?" I said. "I want to see if Woolf can make it, too."

Bobby thought we should go, and when Gabe Paul called back I told him we'd be at "21" at about eight-thirty. Coltin, Barry Price, and I drove back to town, and we all met later at my apartment. The four of us made a seven-o'clock flight to New York, then took a cab to "21." This was Monday night. Bill and Barry stayed in the cocktail lounge downstairs, while Bobby and I met Gabe in the upstairs dining room. He was alone in a corner booth.

We talked for a long time about everything but me—basketball, Bobby's clients, our steaks, old-time ballplayers, Gabe's career as a baseball executive—he started as a peanut boy in the ball park at Rochester, New York, where he grew up.

HAWK

Gabe finally got around to the subject at hand just before they brought in the dessert.

"Come to Cleveland, Hawk," he said. "Don't wreck this trade. You love baseball. Look how you'll hurt it if you don't play. Five other ballplayers, two ball clubs, a major trade hangs on your decision to play or not to play. This situation has got to be resolved and you're the only one who can do it."

Bobby spent a long time showing Paul what it meant to me in dollars and cents to leave Boston. As Paul listened, then suggested nothing new, I started to get annoyed. All he said was he had never heard of a situation like this before, and that I couldn't retire. You'd think the whole structure of baseball was at stake. We didn't get anything resolved except the dinner check, which he paid. Still, Bobby said later he thought the Indians might do something to help make up for my loss of income in leaving Boston.

After dinner, we went downstairs with Paul, introduced him to Bill and Barry, then he left, after saying he'd be in touch with us later. We went from "21" to Mr. Laff's, Phil Linz's place, then to Bill Swain's. We tried to get rooms, but couldn't find anything in town, so we took a two-a.m. plane back to Boston. I got to bed around four.

I was still doing a slow burn about Gabe Paul. He really hadn't done anything except buy us a dinner and try to talk me into going to Cleveland. I went to sleep mad.

At about eight o'clock Tuesday morning Dick O'Connell phoned Woolf at Bobby's home in Chestnut Hill. He was very much concerned about the trade. If it didn't go through, what would happen to it? Nobody seemed to know. When Bobby walked into his office at ten, there was a message to call Bowie Kuhn, the baseball commissioner. Kuhn asked if he and I would go to his office for a meeting with him, Gabe Paul, Dick O'Connell, and Joe Cronin, the president of the American League. Bobby told him we'd be on a noon flight, then called and told me.

"The hell with it," I said. "I don't want to talk to anybody. I've retired, and I'm going to stay retired. I'm not going to New York or anywhere else."

"Hawk," Bobby said, "the commissioner has asked us to meet him, and we're going to give him that courtesy. Now get ready. I'll be right over."

But I didn't get ready. When Bobby arrived, I was still in scivvies, still determined not to do anything. It took Bobby half an hour to convince me I was being a baby and a damn fool. If Kuhn was willing to help get things unraveled, I had to cooperate—especially since he wanted my lawyer there, too. No ballplayer had ever been permitted to bring his lawyer into a discussion with baseball executives—if, for that matter, any ballplayer had ever been involved in a discussion like this.

I finally said O.K. and got dressed. I wore a white turtleneck shirt, a yellow bandana around my neck, a blue pullover, light-blue pants, and white cowboy boots. I looked sensational, but Bobby didn't even comment on my clothes. He just led me to his car and drove me to the airport.

I griped all the way.

"Damn—we just left New York. Now we have to go back. What the hell can we accomplish? . . . Why can't they let me stay retired?"

We were stacked up over LaGuardia and didn't arrive at the commissioner's office at 680 Fifth Avenue until after two. The building seemed peaceful enough—a few people meandering through the lobby—but when we stepped out of the elevator on the twentieth floor, we walked into a hornet's nest of lights, cameras, microphones, announcers, baseball writers, columnists, and wire-service people. I recognized many nationally known figures in the crowd.

Everybody had questions, everybody wanted answers, and we didn't know what the hell to do, or even which direction to turn.

Neither of us had ever been in the commissioner's office, so for a few minutes all we could do was just stand there stammering vague answers, most of which added up to the fact that we didn't have any idea of what would happen.

One thing I do remember was a network sportscaster asking Bobby if we were there to make trouble for baseball—if he intended to challenge the reserve clause or the game's transfer rules.

"We're not here to challenge anything," Bobby told him. "We're here to see if we can't help baseball unravel a very baffling problem."

Somebody finally led us to the right door and into the commissioner's private office. Spacious, beautifully furnished, it was a pretty awesome sight for a mere ballplayer. The five men in the room represented the top brass of baseball and of two major-league clubs. There was the commissioner, Bowie Kuhn, tall, dark-haired, impeccably dressed, towering over everyone. There was Joe Cronin, the American League president, fat, friendly, hail-fellow-well-met, who might be nearly as tall as Kuhn but doesn't look it because he is almost as broad as he is long. There was Dick O'Connell, the Red Sox general manager, thin, intense, with sparse gray hair and a solemn look on his face. There was Gabe Paul, president of the Indians, short, a bit heavy-set, with wavy salt-and-pepper hair, smiling in a worried sort of way. And there was Charley Segar, veteran assistant to baseball commissioners since Ford Frick's time.

We shook hands all around, then the commissioner invited us to take seats while he settled himself behind his desk in one corner of the room. I sat on a chair directly in front of but several feet away from the desk, with Paul on my left and O'Connell on my right. Segar, who didn't utter a word throughout the meeting, sat behind us. Woolf and Cronin were on a divan to the left of the desk.

Once we were all in place, Bobby was the first to speak. He started by assuring everyone that, while he was my attorney, we weren't there to challenge any of baseball's regulations, but to help straighten out the complications triggered by the trade.

He then pointed out what a terrific emotional shock the deal had been to me, because of what Boston had come to mean to me in less than two years. I loved the Red Sox and, in view of the great year I had had in 1968, thought I would be with them indefinitely. I loved the ball park, its short, straight left-field fence making it a paradise for long-hitting right-handers like me. I loved the people, the places, the action, the excitement, the recreational facilities in this truly wonderful town. My children were there, my future was there—and my business interests were there. If I left now, these business interests would suffer—in fact, whatever I did would be costly to me. If I retired to stay in Boston and help protect those interests, I would be out of baseball and my value as a personality would decrease. But if I went to Cleveland, or anywhere other than Boston, my heavy business interests there would suffer.

While emphasizing that I could afford to retire, that I now seemed to prefer retirement to leaving Boston, Bobby pointed out that I was really a pretty mixed-up guy at the moment. I was too hurt, too angry, too shocked, too upset to think straight. Bobby said he had advised me against retirement because he was sure that, no matter how I felt now, I would later regret a decision to quit.

"Baseball means too much to the Hawk," Bobby said, his voice quietly clear. "I don't think he can stand being out of it. He's too young to quit, too good a ballplayer to stay away from the game. He loves it too much."

Bobby paused, looked around the room, then added, "Gentlemen, this man has taken a terrible emotional beating—is still taking one. As his friend, I'm highly aware of this. And, as his attorney, I am compelled to ask you this—must he take an economic beating, too?"

For a moment, nobody spoke. Then the commissioner, the only

other attorney in the room, looked around, his eyes resting for a moment on each of us, and said, "There must be a mutually satisfactory solution to this problem. We're going to find it if we have to stay here until two in the morning."

That was one of the few things Mr. Kuhn said all the time we were there, but it set the tone of the meeting while putting my own confused mind at rest. I hadn't wanted to come. Now I was glad to be there. I hadn't thought there was a solution I could accept. Now I felt we might work one out. I had been a little apprehensive about how these men would take my having my attorney with .me. Now, perhaps because he was an attorney himself, Mr. Kuhn obviously accepted Bobby. There was no resentment, no bitterness—simply a determination to come to an agreement somehow.

As the talk progressed, it was apparent to everyone that this was a special case—one such as had never come up in baseball before and might never come up again. At the suggestion of the commissioner, we split up for private discussion, with Bobby and me going in one direction and Paul, O'Connell, and Cronin in the other.

We went in the wrong direction because we walked right back into that news-media madhouse again. For twenty minutes we heard the same questions: "What's happening?" . . . "Are you making progress?" . . . "What stage are you at?" . . . "How much money's involved?" . . . "Who's doing what?" . . . "Can you come to an agreement?" . . .

Bobby and I stood side by side, like a couple of fencers trying to protect each other against an army. All I did was repeat over and over, "As of now, I'm still retired." As if off in the distance, I could hear Bobby repeat things like, "We explained our position" . . . "We understand each other" . . . "Everybody's trying to be fair" . . . and things like that.

Somebody finally rescued us, and, as we were being led back to the commissioner's office, Bobby told me, "The baseball people are reasonable, Hawk. They're willing to be fair. I know you're emotionally shook now, but it will get worse if you quit. And don't forget, you're tying up five other ballplayers and a major deal."

He finally convinced me that I had an obligation to baseball which I couldn't ignore. The game had been good to me. I owed everything I had to it. The Indians were willing to give me a new contract through 1970.

When, at last, we all agreed that I would go to Cleveland on what had become mutually acceptable terms, I felt like a new man. With the situation resolved, my own personal conflict was resolved. And when, after more than four hours of discussion, we walked out of Bowie Kuhn's office with everything settled, my mind was at rest. It had been a shattering experience, but now it was over. I was no less unhappy about leaving Boston, but I could accept it as the only condition which would keep me in baseball.

When we left the office Gabe Paul made the announcement.

"Ken Harrelson will be in Cleveland tomorrow and, weather permitting, will be in uniform when we play the Yankees tomorrow night."

The next morning I phoned Duke Sims, the Indians' catcher and one of my oldest friends in baseball, and asked him to meet me at the Cleveland airport, where I was due at one in the afternoon. It was a miserable day—cold, raining, dark—and I really didn't expect to see anyone but Duke and perhaps a couple of newspapermen who knew when I was coming.

But I got the red carpet—complete with TV and radio greetings and maybe a thousand people yelling, "Hawk—Hawk—Hawk—" While they gave me the V-for-victory sign and boxers' handclasps, a beautiful blonde in a miniskirt—she must have been freezing—kissed me while handing me a dozen roses. She represented Station WIXY, which has a huge listening audience of young mods—my kind of people. I got a big kick out of the size of the crowd. Man, those people must have really wanted to see me to go out in that kind of weather.

Duke finally got me through the crowd and into his car. The trip into the city produced new thrills, for every time we stopped or slowed down, people recognized me and yelled a welcome.

We went to the Sheraton-Cleveland Hotel, where I couldn't get across the lobby without being stopped for autographs. Everywhere I could hear, "Hawk . . . Hawk . . . Hawk . . . ," and people talked to me as I checked in and as I went to the elevators to go up to my room.

The newspapers had me all over page one, right along with the really important news of the world. One devoted a full page to me —a picture of me in the outfit I wore at the commissioner's meeting, with a couple of bats in my hands.

It wasn't long before the phone began ringing—I guess news travels fast in Cleveland. I answered one call after another, not just from the ball park but from friends, other Indians players, and complete strangers. A few even wanted me to go in on business deals. I referred them to Bobby Woolf. I still don't know what's worthwhile and what isn't, and Bobby continues to handle my affairs.

It's not far from the hotel to the stadium, but we must have been greeted by a hundred people who recognized me in Duke's car. Despite the horrible weather, there were plenty of people on the streets. I had been told Cleveland wasn't a very good baseball town, but you couldn't prove it by me. If everyone who greeted me personally that day showed up at games, we'd have no attendance problems at all.

At the ball park, where the game against the Yankees had been postponed, they showed me my new uniform. While the Red Sox use only numbers on the backs of their ballplayers, the Indians use names, too. When I saw that mine read HARRELSON 40, I asked them to change it to "HAWK 40," making me the only guy in the majors carrying a nickname on his back.

That night a Cleveland station repeated the television show which had featured me in Boston, substituting shots of my arrival in Cleveland and local interviews with me for what had originally been of interest only in New England. I guess every radio and TV station in Cleveland asked for me, while newspapers both there and in surrounding communities called constantly for appearances.

I knew Cleveland pretty well from my many trips there as a visiting ballplayer, but this was different. Visiting ballplayers go in and out so fast they don't have much chance to get around. Superstars like Mantle and Yastrzemski are always in demand, of course, but lesser ballplayers aren't. Now, suddenly, I was a local celebrity, a Cleveland boy known all over the country. One Ohio newspaper described me as a national "household word." Man, I want to tell you being a household word is a pleasure. Being wanted, being sought after, being recognized, being cheered right on the street—that's really living. I loved every minute of it, just as any ham would. And the longer I stayed in town the more I loved it.

Sims and I went to his apartment from the ball park, then to the Blue Grass Motel for dinner. It's owned by Larry Mako and Scott Reed, who treated me like a long-lost relative. I moved in there eventually while waiting for my own pad to be fixed up.

That was being handled by Vernon Stouffer, chairman of the board and chief stockholder of the Indians. He and I got along fine from the moment we met. Through him, I got a top-floor apartment in Winton Place, swanky, new, and gorgeous. Mr. Stouffer lives there himself, so you can see the kind of address it is—the best in Cleveland, in fact. It has a helicopter landing pad on the roof, and Mr. Stouffer told me I could use it for transportation to the ball park any time I wanted to.

Cleveland people already had some business deals cooking for me. Mr. Stouffer invited Bobby Woolf to come and help advise in setting them up. Al Rosen, the former Indians star, now a big man in Cleveland financial circles, will help do some of the organizing. Besides investments, I may have several business interests in town, including, among other possibilities, a Harrelson's of Cleveland clothing store, a Hawk's Nest night spot, and some Hawk Shops similar to what we are planning in Boston.

There were other compensations for leaving Boston. Gabe Paul made me feel right at home. Alvin Dark, my best friend, was my manager again. The club assigned a young guy named Bruce Eglin to help take care of my affairs at the ball park, and a secretary to answer mail that streamed in every day. The Cleveland fans continued to be marvelous, even though my hitting fell off pretty badly after a fast start. I still couldn't walk along the street or drive in a car or be in any public place outside the stadium without hearing my name called or being asked for my autograph. Somebody even wrote a poem about me and somebody else a song. And, just so I wouldn't get homesick Wendell, my Brookline houseboy, came to Cleveland to be with me.

Don't get me wrong—I still think Boston is great. I love the town, keep my pad there, and expect to continue to live there in the off-season. But Cleveland isn't going to be so bad either.

I can still look in mirrors there, just as in Boston or anywhere else. And I can still say, as I admire whatever outfit I happen to be wearing at the moment, "You handsome sonofagun, don't you ever die!"